ST🌀NE MAGIC

OF THE ANCIENTS

PETROGLYPHS
SHAMANIC SHRINE SITES
ANCIENT RITUALS

Illustrations, photos & text by
James R. Cunkle

Ritual aspects, text & vignettes by
Markus A. Jacquemain

GOLDEN WEST ☼ PUBLISHERS

Cover Design by James R. Cunkle & Shayne Fischer

Other books by James R. Cunkle:

> *Talking Pots, Deciphering the Symbols of a Prehistoric People*
> *Treasures of Time, A Guide to Prehistoric Ceramics of the Southwest*

EXPLANATORY NOTES

The scales beside most of the illustrations in this book are based on the "scale arrow" in the photographs. Both are graded in increments of 5 centimeters. For instance, if you measured the image on the left and compared it with its scale, you would find that the image height is approximately 5 "increments" tall. If you multiplied those 5 increments times 5 centimeters (25 centimeters) and converted that total to inches (0.3937 inches per centimeter), you would find that the approximate actual size of this petroglyph is 9.8 inches. While the scale may be shown in varying sizes the increment measurement will remain constant. Each increment equals approximately 2 inches (1.9685 inches).

Library of Congress Cataloging-in-Publication Data

James R. Cunkle

Stone Magic of the Ancients: the petroglyphs and shrine sites of the upper Little Colorado region: the magic of the image and the power of the place: a collection of prehistoric rock art images that still radiate the magic of their making / by James R. Cunkle, Markus Jacquemain; photos and drawings by James R. Cunkle.

p.   cm.

Includes bibliographical references and index.

ISBN 1-885590-04-0

1. Indians of North America — Little Colorado River (NM and AZ) — Antiquities. 2. Indians of North America —Little Colorado River (NM and AZ) — Religion. 3. Petroglyphs — Little Colorado River (NM and AZ) 4. Rock paintings — Little Colorado River (NM and AZ) 5. Sacred space — Little Colorado River (NM and AZ) 6. Little Colorado River (NM and AZ) — Antiquities. 7. Shamanism

I. Jacquemain, Markus. II. Title

E78.C62C86 1995	95-22656
709'.01'130979137 — dc20	CIP

Printed in the United States of America.

Information in this book is deemed to be authentic and accurate by authors and publisher. However, they disclaim any liability incurred in connection with the use of information appearing in this book.

Golden West Publishers, Inc.
4113 N. Longview Ave.
Phoenix, AZ 85014, USA
(602) 265-4392

Contents

Prologue

I remember an evening late one summer day. I had hiked up the canyon south of Raven Site to maintain a section of irrigation ditch which waters the ethnobotanical garden at the Center. This irrigation system was built around the year A.D. 1200 and it is still in use today thanks to the efforts of a small army of hand laborers including myself. I finished my work and started hiking back down the canyon to the site. It had become quite dark. In the shadows of the evening it was becoming difficult to tell exactly where I was in the canyon. I was not sure if I had missed a trail or if I was on the right path. As I moved along the trail I began to contemplate how many others, how many hundreds of prehistoric people had walked the same path, with the same purpose, finding their way home to the pueblo, to supper, hearth and fire, family and warm laughter. By now the darkness had invaded every corner, hidden every stone, and the trail, if I was even still on a trail, could only be felt through my sandals. I stopped, unsure of which direction to proceed. The first rule of being lost is to stop, stay where you are and gather your resources. This simple rule has literally saved my life several times during cave explorations.

I quietly waited, collecting my thoughts which at that moment were the only resource I could think of to gather. During those few minutes of passive quiet contemplation, a yellow moon peeked over the eastern ridge and brightened the sky. Her beautiful golden light illuminated the path, the river and directly in front of me a basalt boulder with a reassuring image; a petroglyph of a shaman with his arms raised in the "prayer/blessing" stance. I knew this glyph, I had photographed it and drawn it and recorded it for this book. I knew which bend of the trail it guarded, and because it was there, I knew where I was and which way was home. I stood there for a long time transfixed with the image. This simple stick figure carved hundreds of years ago still held the power that it was created to carry. The petroglyph marked a difficult turn in the trail and blessed those as they passed who had worked on the irrigation that provided the water to grow the food for the people. I smiled and thought about the many others over the centuries that had received that same shaman's blessing radiating from the stone. — *J.R.C.*

Dedications

To the ebb and flow of spirit through the human animal.

J. R. Cunkle

To John and Donna Jacquemain

Without a firm foundation all houses are destined to fall.

M. Jacquemain

Acknowledgements

We would like to thank all of those people who shared their knowledge of rock imagery locations making this book possible and a special thanks to those who continue to act as stewards and protect the petroglyph sites.

Charles Hutton for his patience holding the scale arrow, enduring infinite adjustments to the light meter and for his diligence in searching the cliffs for new glyph areas.

Todd Bosen and his family for their help and enthusiasm.

Jennifer Jacquemain and Carol Cunkle for their assistance in editing the text. Mark Saylor for his interest and concern.

A special thanks to Jim and Sharon Masterson for their continuing support of the Raven Site project.

Foreword I

Having completed two studies on the ceramics of the White Mountains of Arizona and publishing books based on each of them (*Talking Pots* focusing on the symbolism painted on the vessels and *Treasures of Time* identifying ceramic types and dates), it seemed a natural step to begin recording and identifying the petroglyphs from the Upper Little Colorado River area.

Few of these petroglyphs have been published. A regional attempt to record and document the images is an urgent cause. These petroglyph sites are rapidly disappearing due to theft, mindless vandalism and the bulldozers of "progress".

I began this study using similar methods used in the research of the symbols seen on the prehistoric ceramics. I attempted to isolate symbols with unit meaning. This proved less than perfect. Petroglyphs are often clustered with older images superimposed by newer glyphs and it is often difficult to determine the context of single elements or even clusters of symbols. It became apparent that the context of the symbols was crucial to the meaning. We began to investigate why the petroglyphs were created. What purpose did they serve? We quickly recognized that the location of the panels played a predominate role to answer the question of contextual meaning.

Ceramics of the prehistoric Southwest which display meaningful symbols have a built-in context. They were created and painted by one person at one point in prehistory. The symbols and images are frequently combined to illustrate a story or legend. These ceramic images give researchers valuable clues concerning the life ways of the prehistoric people of the Southwest. This is why it is important to compare these ceramic images to the depictions carved in stone. Throughout this text you will encounter examples of prehistoric ceramics that will be compared to the petroglyph examples. The ceramic examples will illustrate objects and actions that are similar to those seen as petroglyphs with the advantage of more detail and clearer imagery. The ceramics of the Mimbres people dating from A.D. 950 through A.D. 1150 are some of the best prehistoric illustrations of daily life, ceremonial objects, rituals, myth and legend. The images on these bowls provide vital clues which illuminate the meaning of many petroglyph depictions.

The figures in this text were recorded by first photographing the petroglyph and then blowing the image up to five or even ten times the original size. These enlarged images were then traced. This proved to be a very successful method to obtain every detail of the petroglyph image. Very often details that were not clearly visible while viewing the petroglyph were revealed. Now that I have had the privilege of hand drawing hundreds of petroglyph depictions for this text I feel that I can recommend the act of drawing the petroglyphs to other petroglyph enthusiasts as an excellent way to truly begin to understand and appreciate the nature of the depictions. I discovered that only after I had drawn the image did I truly "see" all of the detail and design.

During this study the piles of photographs and drawings almost began to arrange themselves. Like images were grouped with like, and it became obvious very quickly which petroglyphs were depicting analogous ideas and a similar use of sympathetic magic.

James R. Cunkle

Foreword II

Religion is a body of thought explaining the universe and humanity's place within it. Ritual is a tool of religion which serves to direct the forces of the universe thus securing and improving humanity's state in the world. Investigating religion, its rituals, tools, and supporting beliefs, requires more than an examination of the objective evidence. A people's comprehension of the esoteric heart of religion is subjective. Only from the perspective of that personal comprehension can one begin to understand the religious values, techniques, and motives of a people.

As a student of religion, I found it exciting to investigate the foundations of shamanic practice. Shamanism, the first world religion, finds its diverse practice an essential part of the history of virtually all people. The American Southwest, however, is particularly rich in the physical and cultural legacy of shamanism, making it a valuable window to the ritual past.

When you spend time investigating the ruins of an ancient people you develop an affinity for those who built the now crumbling walls. You know they, like you, had triumphs and defeats, passions and petty problems, heroes and villains. You know they were alive. Over time, characters fill your head like ghosts from the past telling their stories. The vignettes, which introduce petroglyph sections in this book, tell just such a story. My intention here was to provide a little food for the imagination to complement the more substantial information. The vignettes offer one possible view of the people who produced petroglyphs and practiced the old forms of shamanic magic.

The petroglyph interpretations in this book are based on our determination of the most probable or prevalent meaning as determined by ethnographic records, explanation (local and parallel), myth, and related ceramic symbols. Our interpretations are not necessarily the best or only interpretations. The nature of the subject makes any interpretation controversial and open to critique. We offer this work in the hopes of bringing potentially new information to light, raising interest, and deepening the scope of petroglyph research.

The "ritual aspects" sections of this book are based on the universal elements of world-wide shamanism and educated speculation. The hard facts pertaining to the old forms of shamanism have been lost to time. In the Southwest, these older forms were superseded by later religious movements such as the Katsina religion. Consequently, the interpretations in this book pertain to prehistoric shamanic religion and do not make public the components of contemporary Native American religion.

Markus A. Jacquemain

Part I

Introduction to Stone Images

WHAT ARE PETROGLYPHS?

Petroglyphs are images created in stone by means of carving or "pecking" the outer stone surface away and exposing the deeper stone surface beneath. Most stone surfaces in the Southwest are covered by a thin layer on the exterior called a patina or desert varnish. This patina is created naturally by the rocks' exposure to the elements. Rain, snow and sunlight interact on the surface with salts and minerals within the rock creating a thin outer darkening of the stone. The prehistoric people would chisel or peck away this thin dark outer layer and expose the original stone surface to create the petroglyph images.

The tools used to peck and chisel the stone surface were simple hand held hammer stones and stone chisels in the case of chiseling, and often just a small round river cobble was used to peck the patina surface. Some researchers have concluded that simple pecked depictions were created earlier in prehistory than those that were chiseled simply because a hammer stone and chisel is a slightly more complex tool kit than is a hand held river cobble. Differentiating pecked and chiseled depictions and associating earlier or later dates according to either of these simple techniques is far from conclusive.

Another frequently observed technique used in the creation of the glyphs is the use of scratching. Often portions of the depictions were created by abrading the surface of the patina with a sharp stone. This was usually done to enhance the glyph with more detail.

WHAT ARE PICTOGRAPHS?

A pictograph differs from a petroglyph in that it is not carved into the stone but is instead a painted depiction on the stone surface. Few pictographs survive the ravages of time. These painted images are very fragile and in open areas that are exposed to the elements these colorful pictographs fade and disappear. Pictographs often survive in caves and under rock ledges where they are protected from the elements. Painted colors often include blues made from ground turquoise, reds from iron oxides, white from kaoline, yellow from limonite, and blacks and grays from charcoal. These naturally occurring pigments were ground into a fine powder, mixed with water, saliva, urine or blood and then were painted onto the stone surface.

It is very probable that many of the carved and pecked petroglyphs were also originally enhanced with paints which have now faded to the elements, leaving only the pecked and carved image behind. Examples of petroglyphs that were also painted have recently been discovered in our survey area. Cup stones, small depressions which were probably used for grinding colored pigments, are a frequent discovery in the petroglyph areas. The petroglyphs that are presented in this volume were photographed from the rock art panels of the Upper Little Colorado River area. This area includes the mountain ranges south of Springerville and Eagar, Arizona and along the Little Colorado River as far north as the Zuni Reservation. Petroglyphs just east of the river are also presented as well as those found as far west as Snowflake, Arizona (see map—figure 1). A few of the glyphs have been previously published, usually with a specific focus such as Kokopelli depictions (Slifer/Duffield 1994) and panels from the Zuni area that may illustrate a specific legend or story, or interpreted using modern Zuni informants (Young 1990). It is exciting to discover a petroglyph panel in the field and then to rediscover the same panel published in the literature. It enables the researcher/recorder to compare their current research with the impressions presented by other petroglyph enthusiasts. It is like finding a published photograph of an old friend.

RECORDING, PUBLISHING AND PRESERVING

Recording the petroglyphs of the Southwest with a regional focus is a pragmatic approach to the problem of classifying petroglyphs. Polly Schaafsma used this system for the entire Southwest and clearly identified many distinctive styles of petroglyphs that are associated with different regions and temporal periods (Schaafsma 1980). These regional or "area" variations became more apparent as we proceeded to record the glyphs from the Upper Little Colorado. Petroglyphs from one canyon in the region began to exhibit overall differences in style, form and execution from petroglyphs from other canyons. It is hard to describe exactly what specific differences exist from one local area to another nearby rock art site and the problem is further complicated by the reuse of the same glyph areas over several thousand years. It is more a subjective "feel" about one petroglyph area as compared to another. One area will illustrate a seeming overabundance of bird, centipede, or geometric glyphs as compared to a rock art area only a few miles away.

One rather distinctive "canyon to canyon" petroglyph variation is that one canyon or area will often exhibit several of the same symbols, usually geometric although sometimes zoomorphic. In a single canyon only a couple of miles long a unique and distinct glyph will be repeated

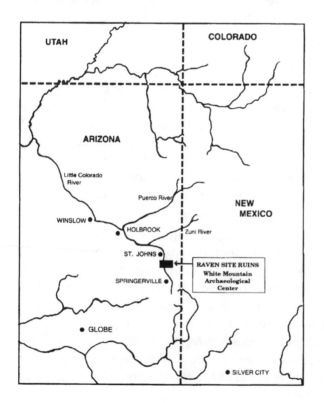

Figure 1 . Raven Site Ruins is located along the Upper Little Colorado River in east/central Arizona and is central to our petroglyph survey area. This area lies between the Anasazi Cultural areas to the north and the Mogollon Cultural areas to the south. This region includes cultural features from both groups.

several times and in several different contexts with other petroglyphs. These symbols may represent different clans and the repeated use of the same symbol in the canyon simply identifies a repeated use of the canyon by the same clan over an extended period of time.

Recording and publishing the rock imagery of the Southwest is an urgent cause. Entire areas that I surveyed as a young man have vanished under subdivisions and highways. Many of the panels that were unadulterated at the beginning of this study are now spray painted, riddled with bullet holes, or destroyed by theft and/or the addition of modern graffiti. If petroglyphs were more portable, I doubt whether any of them would still remain in their proper context; they would have undoubtedly been carted off by looters years ago. During this study I have met many people who would show me rock art areas and exclaim "Gee, I sure wish I could move these things into my front yard." I tremble at the idea of petroglyph panels surrounded by daisies and manicured grass alongside a birdbath and a lawn ornament!

Photo 2 shows a petroglyph panel from south of Holbrook, Arizona. Thieves have attempted to remove the glyph by chiseling around the panel. This always results in the destruction of the petroglyph. The thieves go away with nothing to show for their efforts and an important part of prehistory is forever lost.

Photo 1 shows a petroglyph panel that has been riddled with bullet holes.

A large number of the rock imagery sites throughout the Southwest are located on state or federal lands, and the responsibility to protect these areas falls into the hands of a few understaffed governmental agencies. Many local groups have been organized to assist in the stewardship of the sites and these have played an important role in their preservation. The local chapter of the Arizona Archaeological Society in Cave Creek, Arizona has played a vital role in the protection of petroglyphs in that area. Their recording methods were so meticulous that they are now used as a standard by other recorders of rock imagery be they academics or simply enthusiasts. These rock art stewards are probably the best protection that the glyph areas can currently receive. By frequently visiting the petroglyph sites, touring the panels and recording with photography or drawings, the presence of the stewards discourages those who would attempt to chisel off and remove sections of panels or who mindlessly add their own figures and initials over symbols that are thousands of years old.

STONE ART ETIQUETTE

Most petroglyph enthusiasts know how to behave in petroglyph areas, and the rules of etiquette are indeed common sense. However, there are nuances that perhaps someone new to the field should know. Hiking in remote areas for any purpose requires a set of behaviors that will enhance the hike if they are followed. Tread lightly. Be very careful to impact the area as little as possible. Look where you are walking. Try not to disturb even a rock in the trail. Remote areas will reveal a cornucopia of wildlife and beauty if you are observant enough to appreciate it. Practice quiet. The less noise made while in the field the more wildlife you will encounter and your hike will demonstrate a respect not only for the natural surroundings but also for the people who created the glyph areas so long ago.

I often share many petroglyph areas with enthusiastic school kids, taking a group into the field and teaching them the importance of preservation and respect. I usually begin the hike by having them gather around and explaining that their behavior in the field should be equivalent to their behavior in church, practicing quiet, deliberate, cautious movement, and respect. There is nothing more out of place in the field than a blaring radio or someone shouting to a friend across the canyon.

Photographing petroglyphs can be a difficult process. Bright sunlight is not always the best light for the best results. Bring along a blanket or other device to create artificial shade over the petroglyph that you want to photograph. Try a polarizing filter. A cloudy day is an ally; however, in the Southwest overcast days are rare. Including a scale in the photograph is very helpful for later analysis. In this volume you will see in each photograph a small wooden scale that I made many years ago. It is divided into 5 centimeter increments. Each increment is painted alternately black and white. One side is vivid black and white and one side is a duller, less vivid black and white pattern. This facilitates shots that fall in bright sunlight and cannot be shaded. The duller paint job on one side of the scale will not blast out your light meter. Placing the scale in good proximity to the petroglyph can often be tricky. Usually there is a place in the rock that will allow the placement of the scale. However, having a friend hold the scale into the frame of the picture works equally as well, and sharing your petroglyph adventure with a friend is usually more fun.

Never chalk or artificially surface-enhance a petroglyph. Do not touch the petroglyphs with your fingers. Touching and chalking disturbs the surface of the figure and adds foreign elements such as oils from your skin. These foreign elements could adulterate new dating techniques that are currently being tried in an attempt to date the panels. Never build a fire near a petroglyph panel. The smoke can darken the glyphs and the heat of the fire can exfoliate the stone surface. Even candles and incense can damage these sites. Rubbings are also prohibited. Use your camera or sketch pad only. These rules of the field are the same for all adventures in delicate areas. "Take only pictures and leave only footprints" and as few footprints as possible. Most hikers and petroglyph lovers go a step farther. Not only do they never litter, but they cart out of the field as much of the trash as they can that they find along the trail.

SHARING STONE ART LOCATIONS

Finding a petroglyph/pictograph area with several good panels within an easy walk along a beautiful stream in a high desert canyon is a joyful experience. I am always eager to share that experience. Sharing information about where stone art can be found needs to be tempered with caution. If the wrong people learn of these delicate areas, the images may suffer along with the natural environment. Not everyone you meet may be as respectful to the panels as you are. Many areas on state and federal lands have been closed/restricted because of negative impact to the lands and the cultural resources they hold. Throughout this volume under the photographs and figures of the glyphs, the location will be vaguely identified such as "south of Holbrook, Arizona" or "north of St. Johns, Arizona". I regret the need for these precautionary measures. However, sharing the exact location of the panels could lead brainless and disrespectful people to the sites and could result in damage to the panels and/or the environment.

If you would like to see the petroglyphs up close, the best policy is to contact the local site stewards. The Arizona Archaeological Societies' various local chapters have many groups that may be willing to assist, or contact the National Park Service, the U.S. Bureau of Land Management, U.S. Forest Service or the State Parks. Better still, become involved in the preservation of not only the petroglyphs but also the endangered prehistoric sites by becoming a member of your state's archaeological organizations. The White Mountain Archaeological Center at Raven Site Ruins in east/central Arizona conducts daily hikes from May through October into the petroglyph areas featured in this book.

DATING STONE IMAGES

For many years researchers have been attempting to discover a way to date petroglyphs. If an accurate date could be assigned to a petroglyph panel, the glyphs would reveal many more secrets than can currently be deciphered. Many methods have been tried, and new techniques are beginning to show signs of accomplishing this goal.

Researchers are currently attempting to obtain carbon-14 dates from small samples of pollen from beneath the desert patina that re-coats the surface of the glyph. This is one of the reasons that it is so important not to touch or chalk the petroglyphs. The oils from your hands and the addition of the chalk would adulterate future attempts at dating.

Another method that has shown some success is digging at the base of a petroglyph panel and collecting subsoil samples for carbon-14 dating near buried petroglyphs. The date obtained is only relevant to those subsoil petroglyphs. Carbon-14 dating is not the archaeologist's best dating technique, but something is better than nothing.

Measurement of the patina on the surface of the rock would seem to be the best method to date the panels. After the glyph is carved or pecked into the rock, the surface of the petroglyph slowly begins to re-patina due to moisture and salts leaching out of the stone. However, the patina rates vary from one rock to the next. Even the same rock face will exhibit several different patina rates depending upon how the sunlight strikes the surface, how water runs down the face of the stone and the internal nature of the stone itself.

Attempts have been made to measure the growth of lichen over the surface of the petroglyphs. Desert lichen grows very slowly and this method has had limited success primarily because lichen growth rates vary depending upon moisture and other growing conditions. Also, not all petroglyphs have lichen growing on the same rock face, and even if they do it is not possible to tell how long the glyph was present on the rock *before* the lichen started growing

Other researchers have attempted to identify different rock art styles with different temporal periods by comparing the petroglyphs with other datable cultural materials such as ceramics, or by the petroglyphs' close proximity to a datable archaeological site.

Some petroglyphs date themselves. For example, if the glyph illustrates a horse then the glyph must have been created after the introduction of the horse into the Southwest; i.e., the panel must have been made after A.D. 1540. If the petroglyph depicts a bow and arrow, then the glyph would have to have been pecked into the stone after the appearance of the bow and arrow into the Southwest around the year A.D. 200 and any petroglyphs that are superimposed by the bow and arrow illustration are pre-A.D. 200. Illustrations of corn can also be relatively dated in the same way. Corn arrived in the Southwest, like the bow and arrow, around the year A.D. 200.

One remarkable panel from north of Raven Site Ruins illustrates an anthropomorph (something with human shape or characteristics) with arms spread in a "prayer/blessing" stance (see photo 3). The figure is superimposed over older petroglyphs. In fact, the figure is holding an older "prayer/blessing" stance anthropomorph in its hand. This newer petroglyph was pecked into the stone after the year A.D. 1500. This is evident because the figure is a "sandpainting" image. Sandpainting images are used by the Navajo and occasionally the Apache in ceremonies involving curing and other functions. The Apache and Navajo (Athapaskan speakers) arrived in the Southwest around the same time as the Spanish Conquistadors; i.e., post-A.D. 1500. The creator of this petroglyph utilized the older images and incorporated their power into his/her depiction. True sandpainting images are created out of temporarily colored sands because they must be destroyed after the ceremony, or the ceremony will not be legitimate.

Photo 3. *Petroglyph from north of Raven Site Ruins showing a "sandpainting" figure in a "prayer / blessing" stance holding an older anthropomorphic figure also in the "prayer / blessing" stance. The creator of this panel incorporated the older depiction to obtain its power.*

Migration

The steady, purposeful sound of chanting echoed down the secluded box canyon. A small circle of people stood before a sheer wall of basalt that was covered with an intricate display of turquoise-amber-and-ocher figures and symbols. The old shaman leading the group was dressed in elaborately symbolic attire of fur, feathers and mask. He examined the figure newly revealed in the sacred stone, and when satisfied, set his granite hammer and chisel stone on the ground before him. The chant changed as one man waved a smoldering bundle of cedar bark in front of the petroglyph panel.

With a fine, sweet smoke rising around them, a woman waved a beautiful fur pelt through the air catching the smoke, while an older man unwrapped a bundle and placed mounds of corn meal pierced with eagle feathers at the base of the great stone slab. The shaman picked up a stone mortar banded with a blue-painted river, carefully opened a leather bag and chose a perfect piece of raw turquoise that he placed in the mortar. With a ritual blessing, he used a scoria pestle to slowly grind the turquoise into a fine powder. With conscious, purposeful motions the shaman's apprentice prepared a mixture of blood, urine, animal fat and ground minerals that would complete the paint formula for the ritual.

Hours later, with the warm sun low on the canyon wall, the people walked away, leaving the canyon to the lengthening shadows. The figure-covered wall was home to the bold new form of a turquoise spiral, the symbol of migration, recording a people's passage through the silent canyon. Centuries later, the paints have long faded, the pecked stone figures have weathered and become faded and dark with the desert patina of time. Still, the spiral holds its message, and in the quiet canyon the petroglyphs wait.

Part II

Cosmology & Shamanic Magic

INTRODUCTION

The desert is very kind to its relics. In the forgotten corners of every old ranch are the lightly rusted hulks of tools and farm equipment used in the last century, waiting only for a little oil and care to be used again. When you walk the mountains, ridges, flats and canyons of this stoic land you will find the scattered traces of the Southwest's long history. Tin cans, beer bottles and brass casings speak to us of the turbulent near past. If you look closely, with an eye trained to the task, you will notice those relics of the more distant past. A sherd of painted pottery, a point, or a stone tool can take your imagination back to those distant times and different worlds. But when you turn a corner on your desert hike and find yourself confronted with an ancient stone shrine and a wall of dancing, floating and blessing petroglyphs, you are in one of those other worlds. Petroglyphs are not just inert remains of lost cultures, instead they are dynamic surviving components of those cultures.

The focus of this book is the Four Corners region of the North American Southwest. This rugged country spans rocky, snow-covered mountains to green river valleys and is among the most remote and least known regions of the U.S. For millennia this region was inhabited by archaic tribes of hunters and gatherers who eventually made the transition to agricultural societies and left behind impressive ruins, artifacts and petroglyphs.

Many scholars of the Southwest have compiled books of petroglyphs while attempting to determine their representational meaning. This approach, while valuable, does not look deeply enough into the purpose of petroglyphs. The orthodox means of interpreting petroglyphs is the limited product of narrow understanding, reducing the meaning of petroglyphs to simple representations of particular ideas, deities or clan affiliations. Such scholars give no more significance to petroglyphs than we do to simple road signs or trademarks. However, petroglyphs are much more than what they represent. To their creators they had a more substantial meaning while playing a central part in the ceremonial life of the prehistoric cultures of the Southwest. We must move beyond the *what* of petroglyph identification and begin to understand the context of their production and use, so that we may begin to understand the *why* of their production.

It is impossible to discern the comprehensive meaning or purpose of petroglyphs without first understanding the animistic cosmology of hunter-gatherers and early agricultural groups. Animism holds that all objects and beings have an innate spiritual quality. We must understand that the conceptions of prehistoric people were based on this perception of universal spirit. Such understanding gives us a native context from which we can use the available evidence to illuminate the belief systems that motivated the production of petroglyphs.

ANIMISTIC COSMOLOGY

The world of prehistoric humanity was not the world that most of us know today. The physical environment was similar but the conception of the world was quite different, and upon the shoulders of that different conception existed the ancient world view of our ancestors.

With the rise of our Neanderthal cousins 150,000 years ago, there emerged an advanced state of consciousness, one capable of imagination, speculation and abstract reason. The dead of these people were no longer left where they fell to be devoured by carrion eaters. Instead, the dead were cared for lovingly and buried in a manner that speaks of ritual behavior. At Shanidar in Northern Iraq, a body laid on a bed of evergreen bows was covered with the flowers of hallucinogenic plants (Eliot 1976). It is probable that the altered states of consciousness brought about by hallucinogenic plants acted as a ritual vehicle for travel to the spirit world. There have been many documented cases of such hallucinogenic use by latter day shamans (Eliade 1964). If ingesting such plants brought about another subjective reality, one in which the norms of conventional reality did not seem to apply, then it was reasonable to assume that these same plants could, when placed in the burial, take the deceased to another reality or a life after death.

Over 40,000 years ago, our paleolithic ancestors were using art in the course of their ritual behavior. With the retreat of the last great ice age, pictographs or cave paintings were produced throughout Europe. The majority of the figures are depictions of big game animals. Painted mammoths, bison, woolly rhinoceros, reindeer and others emblazoned the deep protected walls of ritual caves (Harris 1983). The spectacular galleries of paleolithic art tell us something affected the human communities that had weathered the ice ages, compelling them to form a ritual tradition that eventually spread throughout the world.

With the retreat of the glaciers, vast tracts of land were opened, becoming fertile environments for game. The warming lands of Europe, Asia and the Americas became host to a teeming variety of abundant wildlife including the impressive species of megafauna. These impressive animals, including giant bison, cave bears, New World horses, ibex, and mastodon, flourished and offered an impressive food base for paleolithic humanity. Our ancestors seized the opportunity and began the long-lasting age of the hunter.

The most practical way to procure the most meat per hunt was to target the larger species of game. This, however, entailed a greater degree of danger. Hunting a mastodon before the invention of bow and arrow required a sophisticated and coordinated effort by a group of hunters. With rocks, spears, and later the atlatl, hunting teams could successfully kill and butcher the most challenging prey. With improved tools and techniques, hunters were able to supply a larger share of the tribe's diet. The increased availability of meat allowed a shift away from the vegetable-based diet, traditionally provided through the foraging of women, and elevated the importance of hunting.

The paleolithic cave paintings are the surviving elements of ritual practices adopted to support and maintain successful hunting. These early hunt rituals were an effort to control the supernatural forces that governed the hunt's success (Young 1991). The nature of these hunt rituals was determined by the animistic world view shared by hunting-gathering groups from the Paleolithic era to the present (Jung 1959). The animistic world view conceives the world anthropomorphically, attributing an animating spirit to all things. The sun and moon, plants and animals, wind, rivers and stones were perceived as animated like people, having their own power and motivations. The world was woven with the fabric of spirit, the natural and supernatural existing side by side in an interactive and complementary balance.

The anthropomorphic personal spirits acted of their own volition just as people do, and like people could be influenced by worship and requests in the form of ritual. If a hunt was to be fruitful, you had to appeal to spirits of, or those in control of, the game. If the hunt failed or the spirits showed their displeasure through some other misfortune, the spirits had to be placated through ritualized offerings (Frazer 1993). The influence of spiritual beings extended far beyond the hunt or affairs of men. For example, among the Ojibway, women had to contact the spirit forces through a vision quest or childbirth to insure a successful household economy (Grim 1983).

The primary thrust of ritual interaction was with the spirits of animals. Animals were necessary for survival and, from the context of an animistic world view, animals take on an even greater level of importance. Not only do they sustain the people, they are equals. The tribes followed the cycles of migration, using tracks to locate new water sources and edible vegetation. In effect, animals were regarded as brothers and sisters who taught the people and sustained them as fellows in the world. According to Zuni myth there was a time in the distant past when all animals and insects talked as people do (Young 1990). This mythic theme is common among tribal peoples and serves to reinforce the perception of animals as equals to be respected.

Although animals held a position of respect, the tribes killed and butchered animals, eating their flesh and making clothing from their pelts. This killing was not taken lightly; it had the significance of killing another person (Eliot 1976, Campbell 1988). Because of its significance, the hunting of animals was also regulated by ritual tradition. Ritual worked in the spirit world to offer atonement for the killing of equal beings. Rituals would also prevent revenge from the animal spirits of prey killed in the hunt. By honoring the sacrifice of the game and maintaining a sacred relationship with the game, the people ensured the continued cycle of rebirth that supplied game for future hunts. In this way hunting rituals matured from simply trying to ensure the success of particular hunts to maintaining the cycles of animal rebirth that made the hunts possible (Campbell 1988).

The ritual maintenance of cycles of death and rebirth was based upon the symbiotic relationship between the natural and supernatural worlds which was a developing facet of maturing animism. Tribal people began to see the physical and spiritual faces of reality as interdependent. The people needed the game to be provided by the spirit world and the spirit world needed the rituals necessary for their animal members to be reborn and live again. This perception grew beyond the limits of hunt ritual to all aspects of life. Fruit would only ripen and the springs would only run with the proper completion of ritual.

The maturation of ritual within an animistic world view opened the door to a broader role for ritual and brought about the conception of magic. By manipulating the natural world via ritual appeals to particular spirit beings, there emerged a perception of causation between ritual acts and consequent results. Once this was the case, the identity of particular spirit beings could be forgotten or changed while still retaining the perception of magic: the ritual effect.

Sympathetic magic is at the heart of most tribal ritual practice. It is believed there exists a physical or spiritual sympathy between a deity, spirit, or person and anything that imitates it. To make a recognized image of a spiritual being is the same as capturing the essence of the being (Frazer 1981). An image of the rain god acts as an extension of the rain god, allowing direct communication, via ritual, with the god, and having a measure of the rain god's powers.

An image of prey captures the prey's spirit giving the hunter the power to kill the prey in the hunt.

The Pan-European cave paintings occur so consistently, over such a long period of time that they embody the essence of humanity's first great religion. When human hands and abstract symbols began to accompany the conventional hunt images of prey and weapons, our ancestors moved beyond the sympathetic magic of hunt rituals. People began to build a grander conception of the world based on bodies of legend and myth transcending the common experience. The tribes had begun to wield the tools of magic and ritual to do more than just ensure the next meal; they had begun to establish humanity's place within the greater cosmos (Young 1991).

Once the tribes began to explore the possibilities of ritual, simple rituals grew into complex ceremonies designed to control ever larger aspects of the tribal environment. The broader role of ritual and magic in ancient society demanded a specialist. This specialist would have to dedicate himself to the task of carrying on and enforcing the dictates of traditional ritual, while also practicing the increasingly complex manifestations of ceremony and magic. The tribal leaders who performed rituals became further concerned with the ceremonial needs of the tribe, establishing the priest-leader dual role of the emerging shaman (Young 1991).

SHAMANISM

Religion is the cement that holds societies together. If we judge the religion of animistic shamanism by that standard, it proves to be the most successful religion in history, having held tribal societies together for at least 20,000 years. The responsibilities of the shaman extended beyond the ritualized use of sympathetic hunt magic to tribal council, healer, visionary and guardian of spiritual harmony. The shaman was the primary practitioner of the archaic magic that was part of an ancient integrated religion having its basis in animism and rituals of sympathetic magic (Doore 1988). In understanding the shaman and his/her practices, we can begin to understand the petroglyph relics of this practice.

The shaman was an extraordinary character who played an archetypal role in the history of humanity. A lone figure who stood between the people and the mysterious, terrifying and dangerous forces of the world.

The shaman's cosmology was based on the perceived interaction of the physical and spiritual worlds. In the late nineteenth century, anthropologists recorded altar depictions of the cosmos as a horizontal cross representing the four directions of the physical world, with a vertical line bisecting the axis representing the two planes of the spirit world (Fewkes 1990). The four directions were represented on the altar because each was reputed to have its own unique spiritual power. The vertical axis refers to the two realms of the spirit world: the underworld and the sky world. The underworld was the realm of death, a place from which beings and whole worlds could emerge. The sky world was the celestial realm of spirits who directly interacted with the physical world in the form of clouds, lightning and wind. The two spirit realms were supernatural, the homes of mythic beings and magical powers. The physical and spiritual were linked together, influencing the others and dependent upon one another as a unified symbiotic cosmos.

From the context of animism the shaman acted as the spiritual intermediary of the tribe. He would enter the supernatural world to address the problems of spirit which, because of interdependence, manifested as problems in the natural world. The shaman acted as a bridge between the two worlds, drawing power from each. From this axial position, the shaman would seek out and master the power of spirit in order to sustain the well being of the tribe in the physical world (Eliade 1964).

The power of spirit was a transformative one that could bring rebirth, a change of seasons or a sudden storm. This power was very real to tribal people; it acted on all aspects of life, benign as the ripening of a strawberry or as terrifying as death. It was this power that the shaman evoked by way of shamanic trance and inner journey.

The shaman was a master of the inner journey. From the context of an altered state of consciousness, the shaman gained perspective on the state of the tribe. This state was evaluated according to the animistic cosmology of the shaman. The mythology and world view of animism offered ready answers and guidelines for the interpretation of shamanic experiences gained through the inner journeys.

Such journeys were induced through a host of specific techniques that varied from region to region and tribe to tribe. However, they all produced a profound change of consciousness from which the journey would embark. Prolonged fasting, dancing, chanting or hallucinogenic drugs would offer the necessary change of consciousness that made possible the shamanic trance state.

Dancing in a ritualized manner for hours or days, the shaman could actively hold in mind the image of the animal spirit with which he wished to communicate. He emptied his mind of all but the target spirit until his body became an extension of the animal-spirit identity. He mimed the animal, letting its spirit fill him until he became it. From the trance state the shaman could effectively let the spirits fill him, become him, and pass their wisdom on to him. By mimicking the animal, the shaman used a technique of sympathetic magic to open himself to the conceptual image of the animal, allowing it come alive in him as spirit (Young 1991).

The shaman was also able to bring the entire spirit world into consciousness through passive trance states such as those induced through fasting, sleep deprivation, and hallucinogenics. From a passive trance state the shaman embarked upon the internal journey of vision and dream experience guided by his questions, his perceptions and the spirits that filled him of their own volition.

Like a seasoned traveler, the shaman came back from his spirit journeys to interpret the messages of the spirit world. As an individual the shaman arrived at his or her own interpretations according to the lessons of shamanic teachers, personal experience, and the perceived needs of the tribe. These interpreted spirit messages offered guidance and council to individuals or the tribe as a whole. The shaman performed some rituals in a solitary manner while other shamanic functions were community events with the members of the tribe assisting in the preparation of the event, watching the shaman's encounter with the spirit world and complying with the guidance of the shaman (Grim 1983). Such guidance must have soothed the anxieties of tribal peoples and given them comfort in defining their role, and the responsibilities of that role in the mysterious world.

When tribal people regularly engaged in ritual/magical practices to manipulate their world, it was a small conceptual jump to apply the same efforts toward the maladies of the body. This form of magical practice fell naturally to the shaman. Healing was a matter of mitigating negative spiritual influences or strengthening the patient's spirit (Doore 1988).

In healing the shaman started to specialize the techniques and tools of the magical craft.

Specialization produced ritual healing tools such as bone tubes to suck harmful spirits from the body, rattles to call and contain healing spirits and images (on wood, bone and stone) that accommodated the use of diverse spiritual powers. Because plants had their own spiritual qualities, they were used to counter the effects of other spiritual entities. Repeated trials over hundreds of generations yielded effective pharmacological skills among most tribal peoples (Doore 1988).

A person fell ill if they fell out of spiritual harmony. In such cases the patient became weakened and vulnerable to harmful spiritual influences. This pattern of spiritual disharmony is a microcosm of the dangers that faced the entire tribe. For this reason it was vital that the shaman maintained both the individual and the whole spiritual balance.

The perception of the human role in the world continued to grow until it became necessary to maintain and execute a comprehensive set of ceremonial events throughout the year. These ceremonies fulfilled obligations to the spirit world ensuring the well-being of the tribe and the maintenance of the natural cycles of the physical world. There were ceremonies of protection, rain, birth, weather, foraging, hunting, the sun and moon as well as those that marked the passage of youths to adulthood. The obligations of these ceremonies continued to grow, grounding the shaman in the priestly duties of the first great religion.

It can be argued that the ceremonies of shamanic animism were only the extension of an expanding base of tribal mythology. And that the experiences and visions of shamans were wholly the result of physiological, pharmacological or other influences. However, it is undeniable the methods of shamanism provided an abundance of experience for interpretation, and that the shamans themselves seemed more than capable of using these experiences in a manner that was useful and comforting to their tribe.

The religion of shamanic animism sustained humanity from the great ice ages to recent times. In that time it spread throughout the world, shaped much of human mythology, fostering the development of tribal cultures that spanned the globe.

Strong elements of this religious tradition survive to the present. The American tribes of the Sioux and Zuni, the Australian Aborigines, the !Kung San of the Kalahari and numerous other tribal people maintain shamanic-animistic perceptions of the world. More than anything, this fact speaks to the effective, and enduring quality of this archaic religion.

THE RELICS OF SHAMANISM

Petroglyphs

Shamanism has left its legacy in medicine, mythology, culture and religion. In addition to its social legacy, shamanism has over many centuries left us physical remnants, the most visible of which are petroglyphs. Because these figures and symbols were pecked into stone they have survived to taunt our imaginations and mutely attest to the ritual past.

Throughout the canyons and mountains of the Southwest there are spectacular stands of jumbled stone and weather-worn towers of rock. These sites seem to exude the innate grandeur of nature. When you walk through these stands of stone, you easily understand why the tribal people saw spirit in nature and in stone (Grant 1981). The stones have power, they are enduring, seemingly timeless and can inspire awe like the grand cathedrals of Europe. You feel this when you look upon a mountain, when you see the otherworldly figure of a towering mesa against the orange setting sun or when you simply sit upon a smooth boulder at the end of a long hike. Whether this power has its origins in objective reality or in the depths of human nature, it is an important part of the tribal world view. The attitude and legends of the Oglala Sioux are typical of the region; "of all the things in the world rock is the oldest, it is the grandfather of all things" (Eliot 1976). The animist feels the power of stone and has the tools to draw upon it. A well-made petroglyph could be used in rituals over the course of thousands of years with every generation of use adding to the mythic quality of the figures. When questioning the Southwestern tribes of the late 1800s about the makers of the petroglyphs, early ethnographers were told that they were made by supernatural beings (Barnes 1982).

Petroglyphs are the remains of ritual practices that acted within and supported the animistic world views of differing tribal societies over millennia. The role served by these stone depictions was multi-leveled and varied.

Interpreting the meaning of petroglyphs is somewhat speculative, as they were used by a succession of peoples over long periods of time. There are historic examples of tribal groups who did not produce petroglyphs but who sought them out as sacred formations and used them for their own ritual purposes (Neihardt 1932). Specific symbols or forms changed meaning over time as they outlasted one tribal group and were used by another. Ritual symbols are most often expressions of complex themes of belief and mythology, and are therefore difficult to interpret in a comprehensive or singular manner (Applebaum 1987). Consequently, it is important to avoid mistaking the particular symbol for the theme it was meant to express if we want to look deeper into the purpose of the creation of petroglyphs.

Typing Petroglyphs by Function

Petroglyphs can be grouped according to function into four categories; *graffiti, recorders, markers* and *ritual*. Regardless of function, all petroglyphs have an interpretive value. The forms or symbols produced by a member of a culture will convey conceptual elements of that culture. Even graffiti reflects an individual conveyance of the contextual culture.

Because this classification system depends on a basic level of interpretation, some petroglyphs can only be tentatively or ambiguously classified. Also, functions are broad classifications with a disproportionate number of members in each category. For these reasons the sections of this book covering particular petroglyphs are arranged according to form. In order to illuminate the probable purpose of particular types of petroglyphs, the functions of each grouping are noted.

1) Graffiti

Of the four categories this has the least members. It is unlikely that more than a very small percentage of petroglyphs were made aimlessly with little function in mind. However we do have reason to think that, at least in the current era, some stone graffiti was produced (Cole 1992). Among the Hopi there are stories about hapless anthropologists struggling to interpret markings on the stones that Hopi men remember producing as children to allay the boredom of watching sheep. Such stories tell us that not all petroglyphs may have served a purpose other than as a creative outlet for some child or aspiring artist. It would be foolish to think that no one, throughout the long history of the Southwest, made petroglyphs for frivolous reasons. Many researchers are tempted to view many petroglyphs as meaningless because of their inability to uncover any clear meaning of those petroglyphs. Such conclusions, however, are suspect considering the abstract quality of many symbols and the cultural and temporal distance separating the makers from the present.

Contemporary stories about the frivolous production of petroglyphs should be considered in light of the present world view of tribal people. The hold of shamanic animism has been broken as the defining world view of most contemporary tribal people. The traditional restraints against children or lay people engaging in what would have been a shamanic practice have disappeared and contributed to the production of modern stone graffiti.

Most studies of petroglyphs indicate that they were made by a very select group of people for overtly religious reasons (Barnes 1982). Like most religions, the practitioners of ceremony were limited to those who were deemed qualified for these most important tasks. It is unlikely that a common member of the tribe would be willing to inappropriately deal with the spiritual forces that were so vital to the well-being of the people.

Finally, making the type of well-crafted petroglyphs that would last over the course of centuries was a laborious and time-consuming task. Few people would have been able to discontinue their hunting and food gathering duties for this purpose.

2) Recorders

The mundane course of human events is always punctuated with events that merit special notice. For millennia, the people of the world have recorded fantastic occurrences of comets, eclipses, wars, fires, floods and significant social events. The archaic people of the Southwest set pictorial records to stone.

Such events were not recorded for posterity's sake, instead they represented occurrences of spiritual power. From the context of animism, unusual or impressive events occur because of manifestations in the spirit world. An eclipse might be seen as some mythological being devouring the sun. Such an impressive celestial feat would effectively convey the power of the devouring being making it an effective vehicle of sympathetic magic. The shaman might make a petroglyph image representing the eclipse to gain control over the being and protect the sun from future attacks. Or the power of the attacking being might be ritually used to attack enemies of the tribe.

There is a famous petroglyph of a steam engine train wreck (Martineau 1987). Some have argued that this depiction proves that Southwestern tribal people simply recorded events for artistic reasons. After all, what ritual purpose could a train wreck serve? For the tribal peoples of the old West, the train must have seemed an impressive monster, a loud, black steam-billowing creature of great power. Riding the back of such a creature made the white man seem invincible, until a bridge gave out and the train crashed to the river below. To an animist who wished to see the white man gone, such an event represented the just act of enormous power. By recording the image of the wreck in stone, the power of the event was tapped and made available for ritual use. Some power had stopped the train and with the proper sympathetic magic, that power could be used to stop other trains, just as the animistic hunter used magic to stop a buffalo.

Most recorded images were produced for reasons of sympathetic magic. What differentiates them from ritual markers was their basis in historical events. Shamanic animism judged rare events to be spiritually powerful; the potential dangers had to be countered or opportunistically used to the advantage of the tribe.

3) Markers

Markers are figures or symbols that convey a meaning much the way "traffic" or "no smoking" signs do. The symbol might have a deeper or secondary meaning, but its primary purpose is to convey a particular idea.

In some cases a trail marker is apparent by its location. There are examples of markers carved on horizontal rocks that seem to lead directly to the head of a petroglyph-filled canyon or other concentrations (Young 1990). Often there are water-related symbols near hidden natural springs. You can understand the utility of this if the spring is located in a distant hunting or traveling area where people might need help in locating water. Petroglyphs have also been known to mark the mouths of cool caves where soot-covered ceilings tell us of extensive use during some prior era.

Many of these symbols, such as trail markers, would be readily recognizable to the members of several different tribes. Migrations, pilgrimages and trade networks would take groups of people over long distances, passing through the lands of neighboring and more distant groups. In such instances, the travelers would soon learn the meaning of symbols marking trails, water sources and territorial boundaries. Over the centuries some of these symbols became established standards throughout large geographical areas.

The majority of marker symbols were associated with smaller tribal groups for a limited period of time. Many markers are clan emblems (Grant 1981) that marked the ritual sites for clan activity or were used to magically strengthen the clan. Clans also made marks to record the completion of pilgrimages or expeditions such as the Hopi salt expeditions or the Papago shell expeditions (Schaafsma 1980). Other markers were meaningful to the local tribal group, marking sites of significance for reasons that have been lost.

Despite the difficulty or impossibility of determining the precise meaning of tribe specific marker symbols, secondary meanings associated with the world view and mythology common to regional tribal groups make some interpretation possible. The presence of such markers can offer clues to the use of space, local trails, tribal boundaries and other aspects of tribal society.

4) Ritual

The most prevalent type of petroglyph is that used in the various permutations of ritual. The bulk of this book, and the vast majority of petroglyphs you see in the field, are the product of ritual or ceremony intended to utilize the powers of sympathetic magic (Grant 1981, Schaafsma 1980).

The manipulation of those forces that animated the natural and spiritual world was a serious and dangerous matter regulated by the laws of taboo. These laws regulated who, when, and how the potent forces of the divine could be directed toward a socially-sanctioned task. Violating the rules could damage the mechanisms of sacred magic or bring harm to the tribe or individuals within the tribe. An overexposure to the sacred forces could pollute and ultimately kill the unwary (Young 1988).

THE SYMBOLS OF MAGIC

The shaman, as a spirit journeyer and master of the transformative energy of spirit, was uniquely qualified to call upon the most powerful manifestations of the spirit world. To do this, the shaman needed tools that could draw upon these vast transpersonal powers and control them. Ritual directed by the strict confines of tradition and grounded in stone symbols were the tools that the shaman needed and produced in the form of petroglyphs (Barnes 1982).

The worldwide occurrence of shamanism and the universality of many of its key concepts allows a degree of petroglyph interpretation based upon fundamental principles. North American shamanism has many elements in common with other shamanic practices throughout the world. Because of this, the shamanic practices, including the creation of petroglyphs, of the Australian Aborigines and other shamanic tribal peoples, present parallels and clues to the meaning and purpose of even archaic shamanic symbols in the Southwest.

Symbolism gave the shaman a means of expressing and interacting with the ineffable qualities of the spirit world. Symbols and mythology offer a handle on those things that are too large or mysterious to conceive, and in so doing, they open the doorway to the infinite perceptual possibilities of ritual (Beck, Walters, Francisco 1992).

In order to facilitate the proper execution of a complex ritual, the Ojibway shaman would inscribe sacred mythological symbols on birch-bark to act as key mnemonic devices. These were particularly important as the intricacy of particular rituals increased and as the shaman came to practice a greater number of rituals (Grim 1983). Ojibway shamans enjoyed great flexibility in forming the particulars of their rituals, making mnemonic devices more necessary as records of individual shamanic rituals. Birch-bark and other convenient inscribing materials however, are less common in the Southwest. This fact or a greater emphasis on less flexible traditional rituals may have encouraged the more enduring petroglyph-style inscriptions. With mnemonic symbols the shaman could execute the ritual in the traditionally prescribed manner and could hand the ritual down to the next generation of shamans. The stone would preserve the symbols and their arrangement longer than the original tribe would survive.

Navajo sand paintings are contemporary examples of animistic symbols that represent the mythological and spiritual qualities of animals and deities within a sacred ritual context. The stylized nature of the depictions refers to the unique value of those depicted and only secondarily to physical characteristics (Campbell 1988). The symbols evoke their spiritual values like notes of music that can be arranged to "harmonize" into a spiritually powerful chorus. Each sand painting is more than art; it is more than the mythic sum of its energies; it is an interactive whole that has a skillfully designed power and effect.

When examining petroglyphs or groups of petroglyphs, we must think of them as more than animal or deity depictions. They represent the spiritual forces and values of their creators and of the successive peoples who made use of them. Also, we must keep in mind the interrelation between individual symbols creating a deeper and more complex level of purpose and interpretation. The prehistoric tribal people were using the symbolic techniques of ritual to bring balance, harmony and well-being to themselves and to their world. The beautifully intricate paintings of East Indian mandalas offer a clear parallel. Mandalas are symbolic altar paintings of the cosmos and its primary components. The symbolic elements of the stylistic mandala were arranged in a manner that attempted to coordinate the universal circle of spiritual energy with the personal human circle.

THE SHRINES OF MAGIC

Walking through the canyons of the Southwest you will see a lone petroglyph (maybe marking an old trail), or several together like lost travelers far from home. In stark contrast to the isolated glyphs are the clusters of petroglyph panels. Panels can consist of hundreds of depictions by different shamans over different periods of time. When we find such a panel, we immediately begin looking for the rest of the "glyphs" in the area. Often our search will reveal nothing new, despite there being beautiful stone walls in the immediate vicinity ideal for petroglyphs. Clearly there was some reason that brought about crowded collections of glyphs in one spot while there are perfectly suitable surfaces in the same area that go unadorned.

The Pima, whose culture is an extension of the prehistoric Hohokam, are known to pay homage to ancient petroglyph sites (Schaafsma 1980). These sites are sacred to the Pima; they use them as shrines, making offerings at them just as their ancestors did. These petroglyph concentrations are shrines today, in continuation of their prehistoric role.

To understand the placement of petroglyph groupings we must consider the importance of sacred space to animist people. Not only are physical objects and animals filled with sacred power, places also have a powerful spiritual quality. It was a common belief among tribal people that there existed particular places where the fabric separating the natural and the supernatural worlds is very thin. From such places, the shaman could more readily control the power of the supernatural world, or could venture forth into the world of spirit. It has always been common for shamans of all cultures to periodically return to sacred places (Beck, Walters, Francisco 1992). Once such places were located (by tradition, vision or physical impressiveness), the shaman could empower the conventional ritual of sympathetic magic by creating a petroglyph shrine in the sacred space.

To the animist, a shrine acts as a battery of general spiritual force that can be tapped for ritual purposes. This is an extension of a sacred place. The force of the sacred place is channeled into the shrine and manipulated from the shrine. In addition, shrines were also created as nodes of specific spiritual power. Examples of this are seen in panels that tend to have associated petroglyphs. There may be a concentration of hunt images or a concentration of water related images (Barnes 1982). These panels are the heart of shrines produced to control specific spiritual powers. To this day the Navajo use specific shrines for special events (Grant 1981).

The shrine also acted to express the mythic traditions of a people. Centuries-worth of petroglyph symbols and forms, all representing a body of myth and meaning, reinforced the traditional values and world view of the contextual culture. With each ritual the shaman transmitted the mythic meanings of the ancestors, binding the people in timely traditions.

As the shrine panels grew more complex with the symbols of shamanic magic (new glyphs being created as they were needed), the shaman was able to interpret more meaning from the possible combinations of spirit values inherent in the petroglyphs of the shrine. Shrines offered a ready mythic vocabulary that could be used to say almost anything in the language of ritual.

THE TYPES OF MAGIC

The practice of shamanic magic developed over the centuries from simple hunt rituals to a well-defined practice that had its own sub-field and specializations. When we look at the ritual magic as a whole, we can identify five types of magic; hunt, healing, protection, divination, and agricultural.

1) Hunt Magic

Shamanic magic sought to draw from the various spiritual energies of the supernatural to empower the tribe or members of the tribe. Power was needed to accomplish specific tasks necessary for tribal survival. The earliest and most prevalent example of this is hunt magic. Petroglyph depictions of animals were often used to control the spiritual essence of the prey (Frazer 1981). We seldom see depictions of animals that were common or easy prey. Animals like rabbits and squirrels which are very common in the valleys of the Southwest are not correspondingly represented in the petroglyphs or pictographs of the Southwest (Grant 1981). It can be assumed that the hunters of the day did not need supernatural powers to kill rabbits, nor did they desire the cunning of the squirrel. When common animals are depicted, it is most likely for purposes other than hunt magic.

The shaman acted as a spiritual conduit of power, directing spiritual power and control to the hunters via ritual. With spiritual control, the hunter was attuned to his intended prey and was better able to locate and hunt that prey. When predators such as cougars or coyotes were depicted, the shaman tapped into their spiritual essence and directed that predator's power to the hunters, making them more powerful and capable.

The tools of the hunter were also empowered. When a spear is shown to be thrusting into the prey, the powers of sympathetic magic demand that it be so. The prey's spirit nature "understands" that it is called to the cycle of death, that it must submit to the power of the weapon and the hunter behind it. As symbols, weapons have the deeper meaning of their role in death. They are the tools that open the doorway to the spirit-world of death. We understand this feeling ourselves and have similar meaningful symbols in our world, whether it be the arrows on the dollar bill or crossed swords on a coat of arms. Weapons of death have always been potent symbols of power and mastery over the world.

When the rituals were complete, the shaman would send the hunter into the field knowing that his spear was power, that he had some of the strength and speed of the cougar and that the elk he wanted to win in the hunt was connected to him in the harmonization of spirit.

Another means of gaining spirit-power was to appeal to the transformative power of creation. Petroglyphs were used to symbolize and thus bring into the present the time of origins. Figures and depictions that were representative of creation mythology were powerful sources of creation energy (Eliot 1976). Lizard-men (anthropomorphic figures with long lizard-like tails) are associated with Pueblo creation myths and are a common petroglyph figure. By virtue of their association with creation, lizard-men figures have creation power. Creation power, unlike the spirit power of particular animals, is not specialized. It can be used for a much broader range of ritual purposes.

When shamans found themselves working with a greater range of rituals and supporting forces to bring about successful hunts, they began pursuing other ends.

2) Healing Magic

Shamans have been using sympathetic magic for healing almost as long as hunting. Shamans are often better known as medicine men. With the long history of shamanic healing came the maturation of the practice. As mentioned earlier, shamans developed an herbal medicinal capability. Animistic healing is based on the belief that all plants have their own spiritual power and that some powers were better than others in combatting the spirit-based maladies of the sick. This belief system, because it was consistent over time, allowed for centuries of herbal healing experimentation, the fruits of which were passed down from generation to generation of shamans.

The herbal pharmacology of the shaman was combined with a large measure of sympathetic magic. Many petroglyphs such as the bear paw were known to represent the curative powers of the bear (Patterson 1992). With this type of glyph the shaman could direct the mythic healing power of the bear into the patient by way of a ritual crafted to fit the illness. Ritual and medicine worked together bringing the different elements of spirit into the patient to redress the spiritual disharmony that was at the root of the illness.

Different illnesses were caused by different types of spiritual disharmony and required different treatment. Some tribes developed the art of healing to such an extent that no single person could have mastery over all aspects of treatment. Among the contemporary Cherokee, shamanic healing has seven distinct specialties that are acknowledged by many in the medical profession to be highly effective (Doore 1988). If you have an ear infection, your local healer will probably send you to the shaman who is the ears, nose and throat specialist.

The shaman became more than a conduit of spiritual energy. Shamans understood the necessary order of it, and in so understanding, became harmonized with it. In such a state of spiritual harmony the shaman could, with a ritual chant or motion of the hand, send waves of vibration through the web of the supernatural world, changing and shaping the natural world. (Frazer 1981).

All doctors know that an ounce of prevention is worth a pound of cure. The shaman understood this principle centuries ago.

3) Protection Magic

The world of the ancients was one filled with danger, both physical and spiritual. Only the shaman could enter or alter the spiritual world to derail any impending supernatural disaster. It is this wise intervention that constitutes our third category of ritual magic. Shields are the type of petroglyph that most embody ritual protection. The pueblo people used a number of shield symbols that later became a part of the Navajo symbolic inventory (Cole 1990). The shield symbols were used in association with warfare rituals of protection. These rituals were probably used to extend spiritual protection to individual warriors and to the tribe as a whole. It is likely that many weapon petroglyphs served the dual purpose of hunt and warfare ritual. If you can control the spirit of weapons, you are free to direct that spirit, offensively or defensively, according to tribal need.

Protection could be personalized in the form of animal patrons. Every type of animal and its accompanying spirit had particular qualities, skills and attributes that could be called upon by individuals who established a connection to a particular animal spirit. This type of connection was also known as totem adoption. The totem was a particular spirit or set of spirits joined to individuals by way of a personal spiritual relationship.

Animal totems were, in some tribes, assigned to individuals by a spiritual official according to the spirit and temperament of the recipient. In other cases the individual was left to discover the identity of his patron spirit through prescribed practices. One such practice was the vision quest. The individual would depart the tribal community for a day or even weeks, during which time he would fast, pray and wait for the vision that would reveal the identity of his totem. In either case the acceptance of totems was usually a part of coming of age. Once a person had established his totem he would look to his patron for guidance, strength and protection.

The totem offered spiritual protection and maintained tribal society. Those animals judged as appropriate patrons were chosen because of the social value of their attributes; the coyote embodied cunning, the elk bravery. Each individual would make an attempt at integrating the attributes of her totem, attuning herself to those qualities and making the totem a powerful part of her self-security and identity.

When a young person had been assigned or had discovered their totem, the spirit connection was sanctified by ritual. Petroglyphs of animal prints are often totem symbols that play a role in the ritual of totem assignment.

Young apprentice healers would be assigned totem patrons designed to assist the initiate in shamanic healing magic. For example, the Zuni held the badger to be the owner and master of medicinal roots, the wolf to be the patron of medicine societies. Thus they became common healing totems (Schaafsma 1980).

Another common means of gaining spiritual protection was through the "blessing." We in contemporary society are familiar with the blessings bestowed by priests, reverends, and popes. The same ancient principle applied to the spirit blessing of the shaman. Like contemporary Southwestern tribes, prehistoric people sought blessings before undertaking significant projects or at auspicious times of the year when such protective blessings of the tribe were most necessary or most effective.

The hand pictograph and petroglyph is representative of the individual blessing (Young 1988). In many cases, deity figures are portrayed with their hands up, in effect, blessing the observer. Pueblo Indians left hand prints at sacred places so that the associated spirit beings could identify them (Schaafsma 1980).

Prevention was served by the tribe's ability to foresee dangers in the future. Much of this ability was based on experience, tradition, mythology and divination.

4) Divination Magic

As the centuries wore on, the production of petroglyphs left behind a legacy of stone-enshrined figures and symbols for the interpretations of later tribes. The Zuni believe that the oldest stone symbols were produced by their ancestors to convey messages to later generations (Young 1990).

We can assume that many tribal people viewed petroglyphs in a manner similar to the Zuni. There would have to be explanations for the petroglyph panels that were discovered as a tribe moved into new areas. The new people would have the same animistic world view that would attribute great spiritual power to the alien figures. Even if there were few images they recognized, interpretations according to their own traditions would naturally arise. If the petroglyphs preexisted the arrival of the latter-day tribe, they would naturally be attributed to the ancestors who were often believed to have maintained spiritual ties to the living. A perfect example of this is the Sioux traveling to sacred places to read the "pictures" of the ancestors to divine the future (Neihardt 1932). There were undoubtedly many such instances when the Athapaskan peoples migrated South to a land rich in petroglyphs.

5) Agricultural Magic

With the introduction of maize to the Southwest approximately 2700 B.C. (Jennings 1989), the ancient peoples of the region had a crop capable of supporting primary agriculture. Agriculture had an impact on almost every aspect of life. The transition from the nomadic, hunter-gatherer life to the agricultural life demands another set of values and disciplines. The change in petroglyph quality, style and composition reflects this change.

With the agricultural revolution the Southwestern tribes were no longer as dependent on hunting. However, there were added ritual burdens that came with dependence on crops. Instead of mastering the spirit and nature of prey animals, the tribal peoples had to learn to work with the temperamental weather, the threats of insects and plant diseases. A new set of magic rituals had to be developed to fulfill the needs of an agricultural way of life.

Maize began to appear in the petroglyphs of the region. These maize figures in the stone were, like most petroglyphs, used in shamanic sympathetic magic (Schaafsma 1980). The new focus was to strengthen the crops with the life-sustaining power of the maize plant. The spirit of the plant was probably applied to all forms of crops, maize becoming the symbol of cultivated crops and the harvest. Like the cougar acting as the spiritual king of animals, maize became the king of plants.

Much emphasis is placed on rain in the shamanic rituals of Southwestern agricultural people. In the Southwest water is a valuable commodity. The rivers and streams are prone to stopping during times of even mild drought. If the clouds didn't bring rain there was always the threat of famine through drought. The people could still hunt, but with the rise of agriculture came settlement, and the increased population with dietary needs beyond the capabilities of hunters.

The shaman had to work with more than the animal spirits of nature or those plants used in healing. The advent of agriculture demanded that the shaman deal with the spiritual needs of the plants that were the staple of life and the elements that supported them. Rain gods and cloud people are depicted in petroglyphs as they became an important part of the growing tribal pantheon and ceremonial demands that placated it. These growing ceremonial demands coupled with the rapid changes in the tribal way of life were the beginning of the shaman's fall from the pinnacle of ritual power (Campbell 1988).

THE DECLINE OF SHAMANIC PETROGLYPHS

As the agriculturally-fueled pueblos grew—bringing more people into close contact and demanding more cooperative effort, tribal society began to grow more diversified and complex. The increased ritual and secular demands of pueblo society forced the shaman to relinquish ceremonial obligations to other tribal leaders. A direct product of pueblo social development was the formation of social religions, such as the Katsina religion. This religion enforced values necessary for the healthy function and growth of the more socially complex pueblo (Adams 1991).

As a consequence of the social pueblo religions, the production of petroglyphs became the responsibility and ritual tool of religious leaders other than the shaman. A new group of social leaders (usually clan leaders) were responsible for their own parts of the growing ceremonial needs of the tribe. These social leaders became the clergy of the new pueblo-based religions. Furthermore, with the growth of pueblo society, the rituals of the social religion were based at the pueblo kiva. Kivas were large underground chambers that acted as pueblo or clan-based sacred space. Permanent altars were set up to meet the needs of clan and tribe. In particular, the kiva altars were dedicated to insuring a good crop of maize (Fewkes 1990).

With so much of the religious ritual being performed by officials other than the shaman, he became more of a healer and a spiritual specialist. The religion of the tribe had grown beyond the capacities of the shaman. Once the pueblo people made the kiva the center of religious life, there was a noticeable decline in the quality of petroglyphs being produced (Barnes 1982).

With the invasion of the "white" culture, the animistic world view of the tribal peoples of the Southwest was irreversibly altered. Those tribes that survived the onslaught of history saw their traditional way of life altered if not completely broken. The traditions and myths sustained by a lineage of oral history were lost due to the deaths and displacements of whole generations of tribal people. The art of the shaman has, in most cases, been lost to the conflicts of the recent past. And with it has gone the largest part of the tradition of petroglyph production.

Reconnecting

Snow Flint, the old shaman, motioned to his young apprentice. Wind Feather picked up her bundle of tools and approached her teacher who stood near the petroglyph panel. She wondered what it was that so interested Snow Flint. When the tribe had completed its migration, settling near these new mountains, the old man spent days searching the sacred grounds looking for the signs of the ancestors. Now, on this morning, he had brought her here to the ridge of a beautiful canyon and showed her these ancestral shrines.

"The ancestors were more wise than most people know. They understood the power of this place; it is a place of the Creator," the old man said. "Look at this." He pointed to the image of a standing figure that had large hands and feet. "This is the Creator. He takes a different form in this land. When I was very young, younger than you, my grandmother showed me the forms of the Creator and the spirit people of her tribe. I see those forms now on this stone."

"I see him. But where are his horns? Why is he so different here?" inquired Wind Feather.

"Every land has its own nature, so the spirit of that land is different. These differences require the spirit people to take different forms. It is like the deer and elk who change their coat from season to season," said Snow Flint.

"Is this the Great Mother?" asked Wind Feather as she set her bag down and pointed to a figure several paces distant. Snow Flint looked where the young woman pointed, squinted his eyes and replied, "Yes, I believe it is. You have a good eye. Now help me with the cleansing ritual."

As the apprentice gathered wood for a fire, the shaman prepared two small bundles of cedar bark and sage. With his flint knife, he cut the bundles to the length of his hand and bound them tightly with dried yucca.

When Wind Feather had gathered enough wood, she removed a fire-bundle from her hide tool bag. She prepared a nest of nettles, thistle and other kindling. She set the foot of the yucca fire-shaft into a notched pit of the fire-board. With strong hands she spun the shaft between her palms while pushing down toward the board. After her hands made three quick trips down the shaft, a wisp of smoke rose from the black ash that filled the fire-board groove. Wind Feather set the shaft down and gently lifted the fire-board to her kindling nest. She tapped the board and the ash dropped into the nest. Wind Feather blew the ash into flame and placed it in her careful arrangement of firewood. The shaman, seeing his apprentice had the sacred fire started, used a bit of soft turquoise to mark

the two bundles with the signs of the four directions. Snow Flint cleared his mind and let the chant of purification rise from deep within his memory. When he was ready, he turned to Wind Feather. "Instruct the flames," he commanded.

Wind Feather dipped her fingers into several small leather pouches and sprinkled mineral powders into the young fire. She recited the chant of connection, awakening the elements of the earth and water to the qualities of the ritual. Snow Flint went to his knees before the flames. He placed the tips of the cedar bundles into the fire and the chant of purification flowed from his throat. After a few breaths, the old shaman regained his feet and lifted the smoking bundles into the air, maintaining the steady cadence of the chant.

Wind Feather placed eagle feathers in the natural cracks of the petroglyph panel. She was careful to wave each feather through the smoke of the fire, to ensure they would carry the fire's message of connection to the spirit world.

Snow Flint circled the petroglyph shrine site with the smoking bundles and continued his chant. As he moved with a simple pattern of steps around the shrine, he entered the chanting trance that his own teacher had taught him. He envisioned the face of his teacher reciting the chant that now filled him, moved through him, mingling with the cedar smoke. From the perspective of his trance he could see the smoke, empowered with the strength of the chant, sweeping away the evil spirits and influences that had been attracted to the spiritual power of the shrine.

Wind Feather watched her teacher intently. She studied his steps, the motions of her body, his expressions. She listened to the chant and recited it in her mind, adding it to the well of ritual in her memory.

Later, as the shaman and his apprentice warmed themselves near the fire he said. "This new place will be the people's home for a long time. You must forget some of what I have taught you in order that you might now learn the ways of the Spirit in this land." "How will I know? I am a stranger here," worried the apprentice.

"We are never strangers to the Spirit. It is everywhere; it fills us and gives life to the world, to the waters, to the animals, to the winds and to the stones. For a shaman it is like a lover we meet at special times in secret places. If it changes form, it is still the same lover—in different clothes."

Calmed, Wind Feather replied, "I hope it is a good lover. There is nothing worse than a bad one." The shaman replied, "I think it will be. Indeed, it takes a form for you now." In a far corner of the shrine, illuminated in the wavering glow of the fire was the joyously dancing figure of Kokopelli.

Part III

Petroglyphs

ANTHROPOMORPHS IN ACTION, PHYSICAL & SPIRITUAL

Anthropomorphic depictions abound in the rock imagery of the Southwest. Rarely will a petroglyph panel only exhibit animals or geometric designs. Many of these human figures are very minimally created using only simple lines to represent the body, arms and legs. This minimalism is, for the most part, undoubtedly due to the difficulty of the rock media. Pecking or chiseling figures into the stone is time-consuming and tedious. The prehistoric artists often included only the essential elements of the design. This lack of detail makes it difficult to clearly determine the nature of most of the anthropomorphic representations.

Occasionally a petroglyph panel will include enough component symbolism to associate the design with other prehistoric information of greater detail. This greater detail can sometimes be discovered painted on kiva murals or on pottery. Painting allowed the prehistoric artist to include elements that the stone media prohibited.

Prehistoric ceramics often portray anthropomorphs in action performing daily activities, ceremonies, and rituals. Vessels often illustrate legends and stories. These ceramics include not only the actors and objects associated with the action depicted, but also symbolic objects and representations that illuminate figurative representations in other media such as the rock imagery of the Southwest.

It is a joy to discover unpublished ceramic depictions of anthropomorphs in action with associated symbolism or symbolic objects. Sometimes these wonderful ceramic vessels are discovered by current excavation and curation, as is the case with most of the Raven Site cultural material. However, these vessels can also be rediscovered hiding in private collections, or between the pages of the more obscure or out of print literature.

STANCE/POSITIONING

Much attention has been given to the position or stance of the abundant anthropomorphic representations discovered on the rock imagery of the Southwest. There has been considerable speculation as to the meaning of these several arm, leg and body positions.

Rigid/Determined Stance

The generic rigid or determined stance with both arms down along the body of the glyph and both legs and feet on the ground, often with the genitals present, has been defined simply as a male anthropomorph. It represents man. Most of the petroglyphs from the Upper Little

Colorado region that display anthropomorphs include other more complex elements such as three toes or fingers, exaggerated hands or feet and other limb positioning that reveals more about the nature of the glyph. The simple rigid "man" petroglyph is rare.

Prayer/Blessing Stance

The most frequently encountered anthropomorphic stance is the "prayer/blessing" position with both arms raised to the heavens and both feet down to the ground. These depictions often include figures with three fingers and/or toes and they may represent shaman in prayer, blessing or revelation (Dunne 1968, Hodge 1907, Waters 1963, et al).

Waving

Several petroglyphs along the Little Colorado River have been photographed that show anthropomorphs with one hand held up as if they were waving. Often the other hand is not present in the depiction (probably because it is not necessary to convey the meaning of the illustration). This gesturing has been interpreted as a storyteller summoning his or her audience, a shaman communicating with the sky, or Great Spirit, and a peaceful beckoning to a person far away (Apostolides 1984, Corbusier 1886, Vastokas and Vastokas 1973 [Patterson 1992]).

Vortex Floating

Human figures are also represented with one arm up and one down; and one leg up and one down, or depicted with the legs splayed upwards. These positions have been interpreted as persons floating, traveling during a spiritual trek, and moving through the vortex from one realm of existence to another. Legs are not necessary in the spirit world. Other figures found on the rock imagery illustrate anthropomorphs in stances that may depict a ceremonial dance. Lines of human figures holding hands in what appears to be dance lines are a frequent discovery. Often Kokopelli or other flute players appear to be merrily dancing as they play their instruments.

Photos 4 and 5. Petroglyphs from the Upper Little Colorado region showing anthropomorphs that appear to be waving. The figure to the right displays only the single waving arm and hand. Deletion of unnecessary elements of a petroglyph depiction are commonly observed.

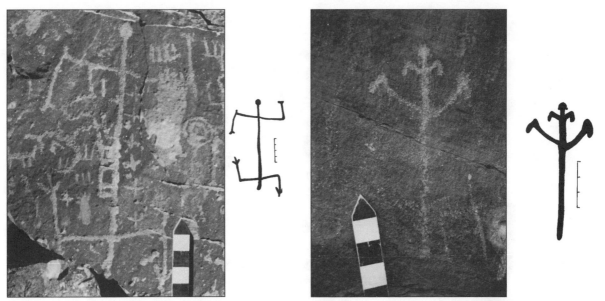

Photos 6 and 7. *Petroglyphs from south of Raven Site Ruins showing anthropomorphs in the floating or vortex travel stance. These figures are often accompanied by depictions of the spiral or concentric circles indicating the door, gateway, sky window, or sipapu leading from one level of existence to another.*

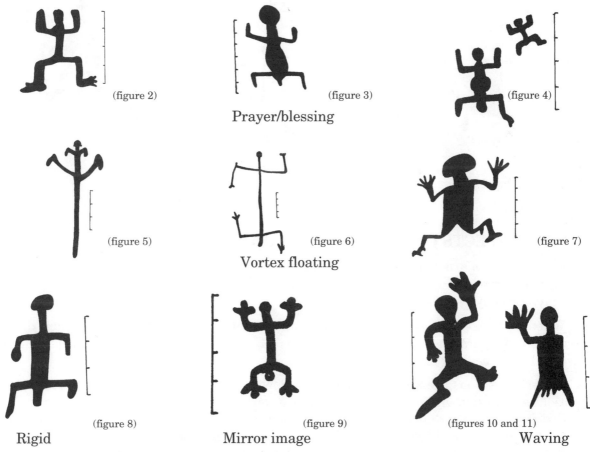

(figure 2)

(figure 3)
Prayer/blessing

(figure 4)

(figure 5)

(figure 6)
Vortex floating

(figure 7)

(figure 8)
Rigid

(figure 9)
Mirror image

(figures 10 and 11)
Waving

Figures 2-11. *Petroglyphs from the Upper Little Colorado region in east/central Arizona showing anthropomorphs in various stances.*

(figure 12)

(figure 13)

(figure 14)

Possible dance figures.

(figure 15)

(figure 16)

(figure 17)

(figure 18)

(figure 19)

(figure 20)

Figures 12-20. Petroglyphs from the Upper Little Colorado region in east/central Arizona showing anthropomorphs with unusual features and stances.

RITUAL ASPECTS OF ANTHROPOMORPHIC STANCE

The position of arms and legs of anthropomorphs speaks to the condition of the being and the spiritual action of the being. We can make general assumptions about the specifics of petroglyphic body language.

When a petroglyph was made, the shaman depicted the figures according to their desired purpose in ritual. With this in mind we can identify several types of body positions that may have had some bearing on the figure's ritual use.

General positions are those with the arms down and the legs showing little action. Such positions are passive with little importance placed on body action or the position of limbs. Most general figures (those that are not specific individuals) will have a passive stance. Without unique features, these figures probably represented classes of beings who had collective forms of power useful in shamanic ritual. The body position of a unique or specific figure was secondary to its mythological power.

Hands-up positions can be passive, especially those with little hand detail, or can be active depictions of blessing or prayer. Most anthropomorphs that show hand detail are mythical individuals or deities. These individuals are spiritually powerful beings having the ability to convey blessings. The single hand-up position can also be a blessing or a greeting. Blessings would empower the shaman or could be used by the shaman to give spiritual power to another member of the tribe.

Some figures seem to be leaping or dancing. These figures express an exuberance of spirit that makes them very personable. A joyous figure is not only easier for people to relate to, but may have, according to the shamanic view, related to the people better. The dancing Kokopelli is a comforting figure who, in his joyfulness, seems to embody the best of living in a difficult world. The shaman would have used these glyphs to appeal to these joyous beings on behalf of the tribe.

Vortex, or floating figures, have limbs in unnatural positions that seem at odds with gravity or the mechanics of standing in this world. These figures are associated with the spirit world and the spiritual vortex that connects the physical world with the supernatural spirit worlds. Vortex figures are floating in the spirit world as natives of that world or as shamans traveling to the spirit world. The shaman may have used these figures to connect with specific beings in the spirit world or may have used the power of such figures to journey into the spirit world.

EXAGGERATED HANDS AND FEET, THREE-FINGERED, THREE-TOED

Many of the anthropomorphic depictions found on the rock imagery of the Southwest illustrate anthropomorphs with exaggerated hands and/or feet. These depictions are believed to represent the Creator from the mythology of many Southwestern Indian groups. Depictions of shamans or holy men are often identified by specific hand or feet posturing or form, specifically the "prayer/blessing" stance and by the frequent appearance of three toes or fingers. This apparently originates from the pueblo Indians creation myth. Before humankind emerged to this level of existence, the people had webbed hands and feet, tails, and genitals on top of their heads. "They were made human by the twins (Twin War Gods). They were washed, their tails were cut off, their webbed digits were separated." (Young 1988).

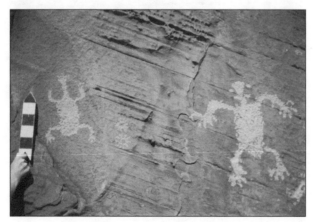 

Photo 8. Petroglyph from south of Holbrook, Arizona showing anthropomorphs with exaggerated hands and feet.

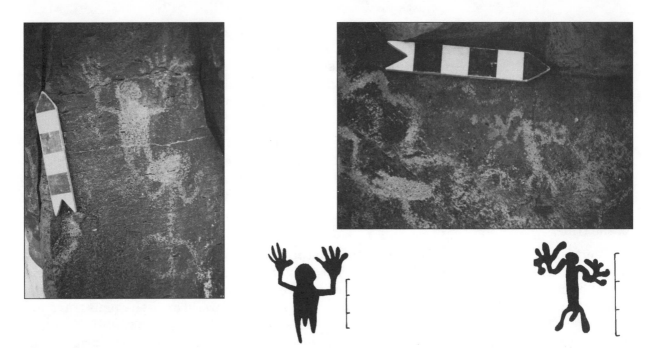

Photos 9 (left) and 10 (right). Petroglyphs from west of Eagar, Arizona and north of Raven Site Ruins in east/central Arizona showing anthropomorphs with large, exaggerated hands.

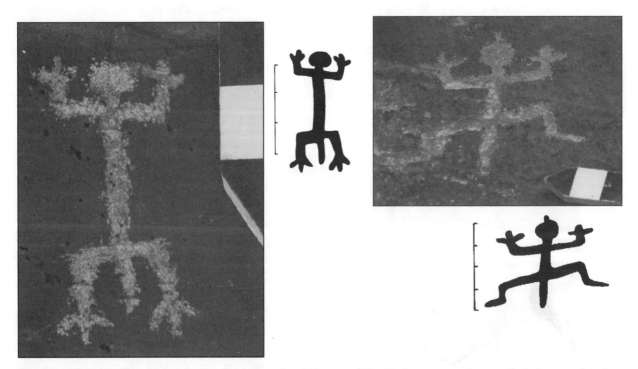

Photos 11 and 12. Petroglyphs from north of Raven Site Ruin in east/central Arizona showing anthropomorphs in a "prayer/blessing" stance with three fingers and three toes and possibly a tail. These depictions probably reflect the pueblo creation myth and these anthropomorphs may represent shamans. The petroglyph on the right may be exhibiting the "genitals on top of their heads" as related in the creation myth of the Zuni.

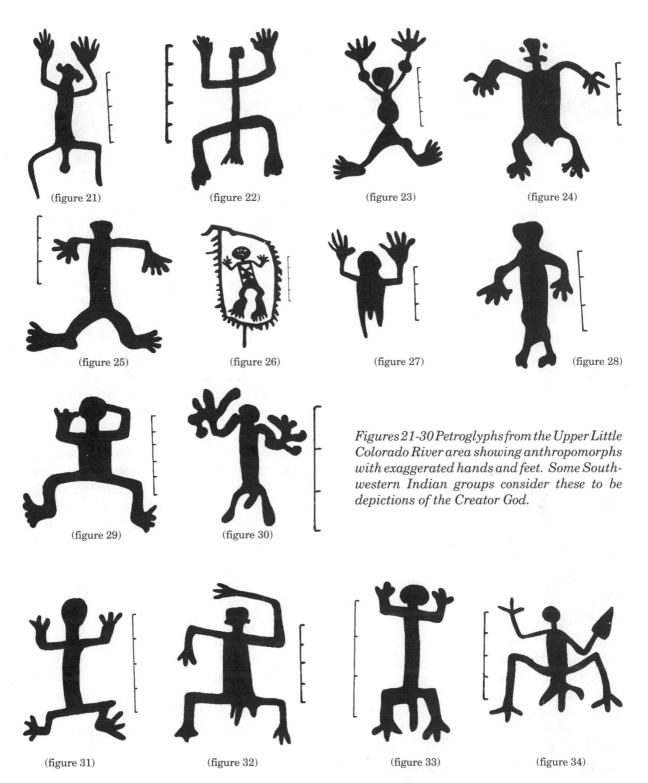

(figure 21)

(figure 22)

(figure 23)

(figure 24)

(figure 25)

(figure 26)

(figure 27)

(figure 28)

(figure 29)

(figure 30)

Figures 21-30 Petroglyphs from the Upper Little Colorado River area showing anthropomorphs with exaggerated hands and feet. Some Southwestern Indian groups consider these to be depictions of the Creator God.

(figure 31)

(figure 32)

(figure 33)

(figure 34)

Figures 31-34. Petroglyphs from east/central Arizona showing anthropomorphs with three fingers and three toes, many in the prayer/blessing stance. These images may depict the creation myth of the pueblo people.

(Continued on next page)

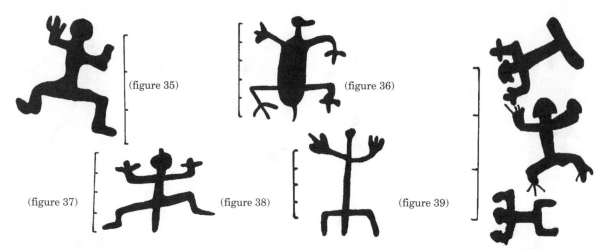

(figure 35)

(figure 36)

(figure 37)

(figure 38)

(figure 39)

(Continued from previous page)
Petroglyphs from east / central Arizona showing anthropomorphs with three fingers and three toes, many in the prayer / blessing stance. These images may depict the creation myth of the pueblo people.

RITUAL ASPECTS OF ANTHROPOMORPHS WITH LARGE HANDS/FEET

Because of the limitation of petroglyph depictions, it is occasionally difficult to differentiate between the variety of human figures and animal figures. The lizard for instance, is depicted in ways that are very similar to some human figures. The similarity of these depictions was not a hindrance to the shaman who had a well-established understanding of the symbolic quality of the petroglyphs used in ritual.

General anthropomorphic images are indistinct representations meant to work with the general collective energies having origins with the entire class of beings represented. Some figures such as stick-figure humanoids with tails, called lizard-men, are general figures. A lizard-man depiction is not symbolic of any particular lizard-man, instead was used to employ the spiritual energy that had its origin in the class of lizard-men. The same is true when the pueblo Indians use corn meal in kiva rituals. They are using the energy of corn in general, not of a particular ear of corn.

The instances where the identity of the petroglyph depiction is important are those where the shaman is trying to use the power of a specific being. These beings would be particular gods or mythic figures who tend to be attributed with powerful, specialized abilities.

Mythical individuals could not be confused with general classes of beings. They had to be differentiated from general petroglyph depictions. Large hands and feet are known to the pueblo people to represent beings with special or sacred powers. These figures are generally humanoid (probably having their origins in ancestral heroes) with exaggerated human qualities. Beings that are not humanoid will generally be depicted with several distinctly non-humanoid qualities. These qualities (horns and tails, etc.) are often taken from the physical attributes of animals.

Anthropomorph figures with large hands and feet are portrayals of specific beings, differentiated from the general classes of mythical beings. The shaman would ritually deal with individual beings in a different manner than classes of beings. Individuals could be appealed to directly. Instead of boldly usurping the being's power, the shaman would make an effort to compel the being into action on behalf of the tribe.

FEMALE FIGURES AND SYMBOLS

Petroglyphs that represent females are less frequent among the rock images of the Southwest than are their male counterparts. This may be because males created most of the petroglyphs either during a hunting expedition, vision quest, or other spiritual activities.

Female depictions are usually easy to identify. The head of the figure will include the circular hair whorls commonly used by many pueblo groups at time of contact. This cultural hair styling was obviously used prehistorically. Female depictions can also be identified by the context of the glyph as in the case of petroglyphs where figures are giving birth. Often the genitals of an anthropomorphic figure will reveal the sex of the figure. Males are commonly depicted with the penis included and female figures occasionally illustrate the vulva. Representations of breasts are rare in the rock imagery of the Southwest. Mimbres ceramics clearly illustrate both male and female figures including genitals and breasts although these representations are usually sexually identified more readily by dress or hair styles. Interestingly, the Mimbres ceramic illustrations indicate that the Mimbres women did not wear their hair in the circular whorls.

The hair whorls or disks that often identify a female figure were reduced to symbolic form. The "mana" or virgin sign is the Maltese cross according to Hopi informants at the end of the 19th Century.

"...(the Maltese cross)..is a conventional development of a more common emblem of maidenhood, the form in which the maidens wear their hair, arranged as a disk of 3 or 4 inches diameter upon each side of the head." (Stephen 1890 [from Patterson 1994]).

This mana or maiden's symbol is often in context with symbols that represent germination or fertility. There are many petroglyphs that have been identified as representations of the vulva. There is some confusion whether these glyphs are, in fact, vulvae or germination symbols, both sharing many common elements. It is not difficult to imagine the symbolic association between a germination/fertility petroglyph and one that represents the vulva.

Interestingly, men's hair styles prehistorically were also conventionalized into the symbol form of the club or cue, and male depictions can often be identified by this hourglass symbol. The male hair cue is also easily identified on the Mimbres ceramic illustrations.

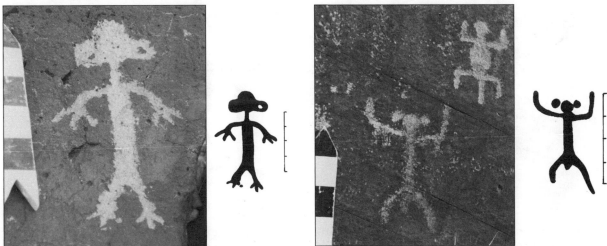

Photos 13 and 14. Petroglyphs from north of St. Johns, Arizona showing female figures identified by the hair whorls on either side of the head.

Photo 15. Petroglyph from north of St. Johns, Arizona showing a rather massive figure that appears to have the female hair whorls.

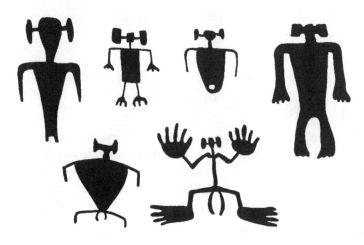

Figure 40. Petroglyphs and Pictographs from Canyon de Chelly and Canyon del Muerto, Arizona showing female figures. Notice the similarity between Photo 15 and the massive female representation top right. (Grant 1978).

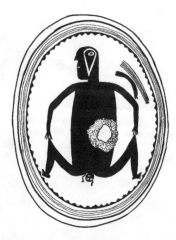 

Figure 41 (left) and 42 (right). Figure 41 is a Mimbres Black-on-white bowl from the Swarts Ruin showing childbirth. Notice her sash and another article of clothing laid off to the top right of the depiction (Brody 1977). Figure 42 is a petroglyph from Owl Springs, AZ depicting birth "..if the headdress (hairdo) conforms to modern Hopi custom, she was unmarried" (Ritter/Ritter 1973 [From Patterson 1992]).

Photo 16. Hopi maiden showing hair whorls (Photograph by E. Curtis, c1908).

Figure 43. Maltese cross representing the maiden or virgin according to Hopi informants late in the 19th Century. This symbol is believed to represent the hair whorls worn by unmarried girls. (Stephen 1890 [Patterson 1994]).

Figure 44. Mimbres Black-on-white bowl dating between A.D. 950 and A.D. 1150 showing two male figures with the distinctive hair cue. This cue was stylized into an hourglass symbol indicating "male". (Brody 1983).

Figure 45. Payupki Polychrome olla dating between A.D. 1680 and 1780 showing the club or cue male hairdo symbol. (Stephen 1890 [Patterson 1994]).

Figure 46. Mimbres Black-on-white bowl dating between A.D. 950 and A.D. 1150 showing distinctive female figures. Females in Mimbres art are often more readily identified by dress, i.e., the distinctive sash worn around the waist. (Moulard 1984).

Photo 17. Petroglyph from north of Raven Site Ruins in east/central Arizona showing the vulva representation.

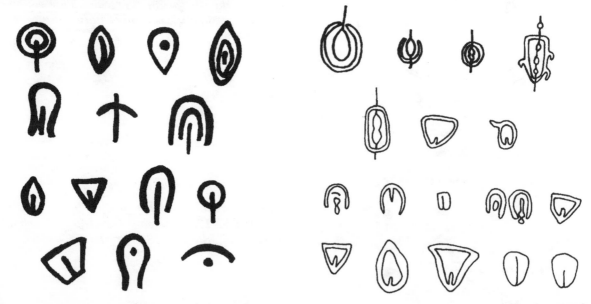

Figure 47. Several vulva rock imagery representations from Chalfont, California (Vuncannon 1985) and around the world (Vastokas and Vastokas 1973).

(figure 48)

Photo 18 and Figure 48. Photo 18 is a petroglyph from south of Raven Site Ruins in east / central Arizona which may depict a sprouting corn symbol. It is often difficult to distinguish between germination glyphs and those that illustrate the vulva. Figure 48 is a ceramic design from the late 19th Century that has been interpreted by the Hopi as the symbol for "maidens locks" or a female symbol. This figure also resembles many of the icons that represent germination (Stephen 1890 [Patterson 1994]).

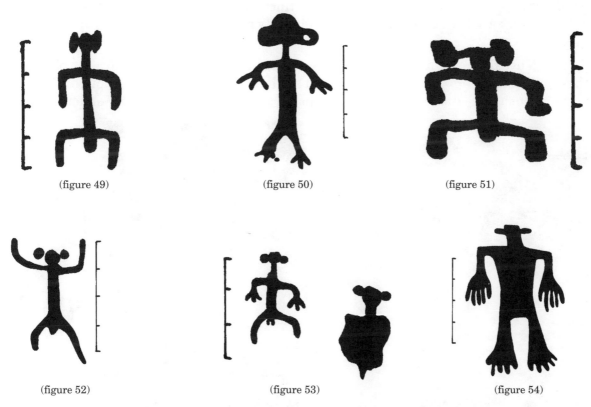

(figure 49)   (figure 50)   (figure 51)

(figure 52)   (figure 53)   (figure 54)

Figure 49-54. Petroglyphs from the Upper Little Colorado River area illustrating females.

RITUAL ASPECTS OF FEMALE FIGURES

Female petroglyphs are, by nature, never general class figures. Petroglyph representations that show gender characteristics are almost always specific beings. These beings are legendary or mythological figures that have known values and traits.

Female figures are often associated with fertility and childbirth. A shaman would appeal to the feminine deities to ensure safe childbirth for expectant mothers. This was a form of protective magic that ameliorated a difficult and often dangerous event.

The Great Mother deity has been a central figure in tribal religion since the ice age. This figure has maintained a central position in the culture of many tribal people to the present day. Many of the female depictions we see on stone walls may have been some manifestation of the Great Mother. The Great Mother was mythically tied to the time of creation, the birth of the world in which she played the central role. Because of this association, the shaman could use female glyphs to direct the power of creation or could appeal to the specific powers of female deities.

With the rise of agriculture, female figures were also associated with crop fertility. Crops were born of the soil as children were born of women. It was thought that female deities could safeguard the germination of crops just as they safeguarded childbirth.

KOKOPELLI AND FLUTE PLAYERS

The most celebrated prehistoric anthropomorph in the Southwest is, of course, the humpbacked flute player, Kokopelli. Several distinct characteristics are used to create this individual on rock art, kiva murals, ceramics and pretty much anywhere symbols and imagery survive.

Kokopelli usually has a humpback or backpack. Some legends describe him as an old man, hunched over, and others describe a pack full of seeds, trade items, or gaming pieces. One of the original pueblo creation stories includes an old man who returns to the underworld to

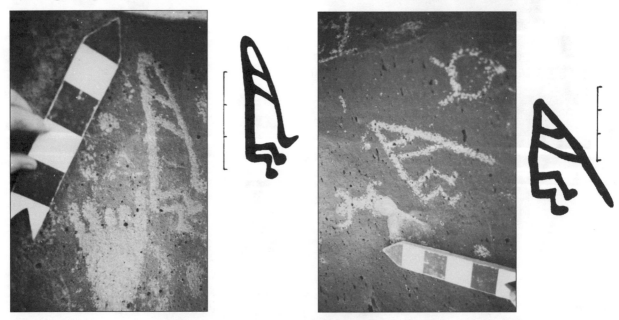

Photos 19 and 20. Petroglyphs from west of Eagar, Arizona showing stick figure anthropomorphs playing flutes. These figures display only the flute and no other distinctive Kokopelli attributes.

retrieve seeds that the people had foolishly left behind. Many of the stories describe Kokopelli as a trader from the south carrying exotic goods from Mesoamerica north to the pueblos of the Southwest.

The flute is Kokopelli's trademark. Petroglyphs show a variety of flute players some with humpbacks and some without. Flutes were commonly made and used during prehistoric pueblo activities and several fine examples have been excavated from Raven Site Ruins. Many of these still play after being buried for over 700 years. Most petroglyph researchers will classify any anthropomorph with a flute to the Kokopelli cluster, whether the image displays a humpback or not. May of these images carved in stone may, in fact, be simply a person playing a flute and not necessarily Kokopelli. Very interestingly, there are many ceramic depictions of Kokopelli found on the ceramics of the Mimbres dating between A.D. 950 and A.D. 1150. None of these illustrations include Kokopelli's famous flute.

The third most obvious Kokopelli characteristic is his often present erection. There are many anthropomorphic depictions throughout the Southwest which display erections, and are not Kokopelli.

A club foot is also a physical characteristic that is associated with the Kokopelli images. The humpback, club feet, spinal deformity and permanent erection may be symptoms of Pott's disease, a type of tuberculosis (Webb, Alpert, Wellmann (Slifer/Duffield 1994]).

Many of the Kokopelli images display insect qualities (most notably antennae.) The humpback is also associated with the katydid and the locust, patron of the Hopi Flute Society. The grey desert robber fly is another insect that is identified with Kokopelli. This insect is notorious for its vigorous copulation and Kokopelli is often associated with fertility (Slifer/Duffield 1994).

Photos 21 and 22. Petroglyphs from south of Holbrook, Arizona showing anthropomorphs (with erections) playing flutes.

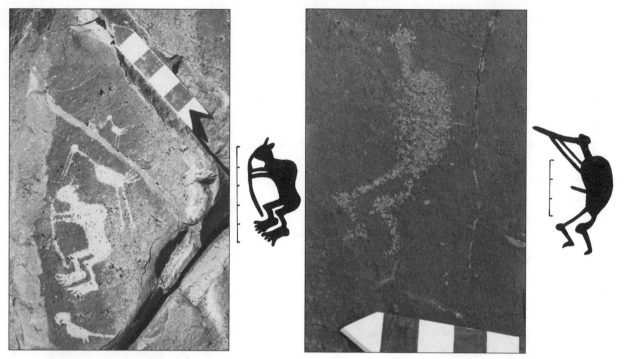

Photos 23 and 24. Petroglyphs from the Raven Site area in east/central Arizona showing figures that display all of the Kokopelli characteristics including humpback, flute, and erection. Photo 24 also depicts the characteristic of "knobby knees" which may be another physical deformity associated with Kokopelli.

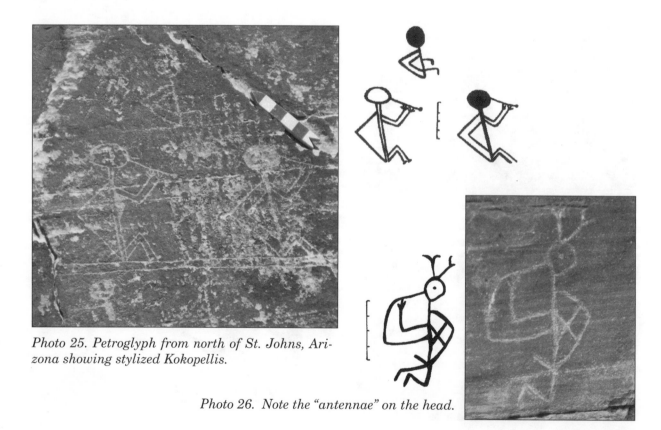

Photo 25. Petroglyph from north of St. Johns, Arizona showing stylized Kokopellis.

Photo 26. Note the "antennae" on the head.

Kokopelli has been identified as a trader, fertility symbol, roving minstrel, seducer of maidens, rain priest, magician and trickster. Prehistoric images of flute players appear in the rock imagery of the Southwest as early as A.D. 500, but these are non-phallic and do not exhibit humpbacks. These early images are probably just people playing flutes. After about A.D. 1000 depictions of Kokopelli with all of his unique characteristics can be found in rock imagery and ceramic assemblages up until approximately A.D. 1350-1400. During the 14th century the Katsina Cult developed among the pueblos of the Southwest and representations of Kokopelli seem to diminish after this new religion was embraced. The name Kokopelli is a combination of Hopi/Zuni translated as "Katsina-hump" and a Kokopelli in Katsina form did survive from prehistoric images into modern Katsina practice.

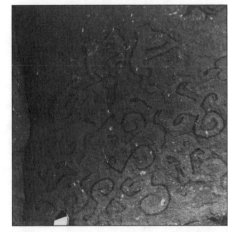

Photo 27. Pictograph from a shrine site south of Holbrook, Arizona showing a very unique depiction of Kokopelli intermingled with geometric forms. Pictographs rarely survive in open areas.

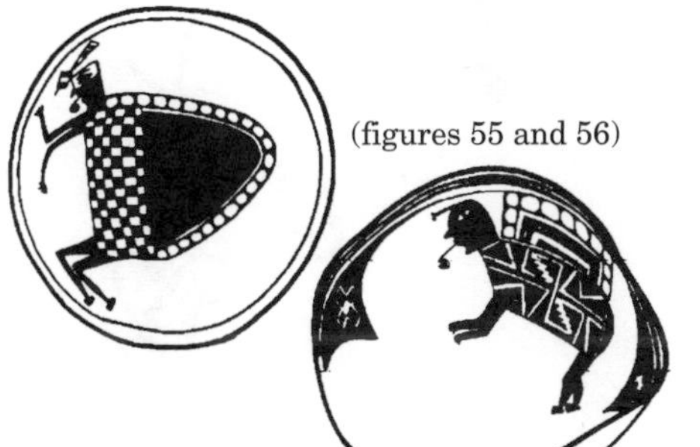

(figures 55 and 56)

(figures 57 and 58)

(figure 59)

Figures 55 and 56. Mimbres ceramics dating from A.D. 950 to A.D. 1150 illustrating Kokopelli with insect-like tongue and antenna. Notice the large dotted hump or backpack / basket in both examples. These vessels have been interpreted as illustrations of Kokopelli. However, they may actually be depicting butterflies with anthropomorphic qualities. The "humpback" on these vessels may in fact represent wings (Brody 1977 and Moulard 1984).

Figures 57 and 58. Mimbres ceramic bowls dating from A.D. 950 to A.D. 1150.

Figure 57. A male anthropomorph with a burden basket and phallic staff. He is identified as male by his hair cue. This may not be a depiction of Kokopelli. The example serves to illustrate the confusion between Kokopelli's hump and the backpack / burden basket. (Brody 1977).

Figure 58 shows a humpbacked male with another anthropomorph riding on the hump. Kokopelli petroglyph depictions sometimes include another anthropomorphic figure riding piggyback on the hump (Brody 1983).

Figure 59. Mimbres Black-on-white ceramic bowl dating from A.D. 950 to A.D. 1150. This depiction is the most graphic known illustration of Kokopelli. It includes the humpback, erection and a crook or staff. Interestingly, none of the Mimbres Kokopelli depictions include the flute (Brody 1977).

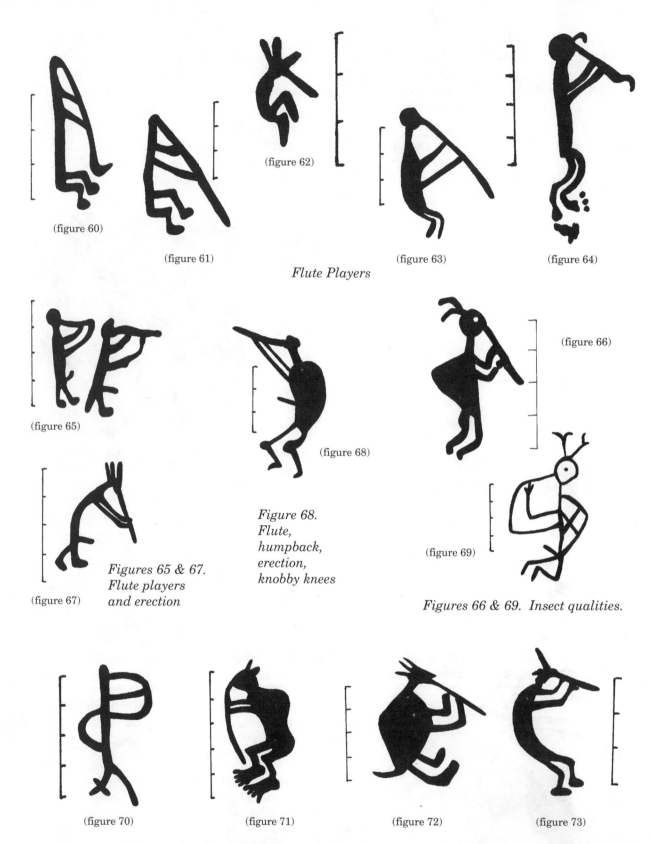

(figure 60)

(figure 61)

(figure 62)

(figure 63)

(figure 64)

Flute Players

(figure 65)

(figure 66)

(figure 67)

*Figures 65 & 67.
Flute players
and erection*

*Figure 68.
Flute,
humpback,
erection,
knobby knees*

(figure 68)

(figure 69)

Figures 66 & 69. Insect qualities.

(figure 70)

(figure 71)

(figure 72)

(figure 73)

Figure 60-73. Kokopelli and flute player petroglyphs from the Upper Little Colorado region.

(Continued on next page)

(Continued from previous page)

Figures 74-76. Kokopelli and flute player petroglyphs from the Upper Little Colorado region.

RITUAL ASPECTS OF KOKOPELLI

Kokopelli was a character embraced by a wide range of tribal people over a large geographical region. He was associated with a rich mythic lore that has matured over the centuries reflecting the depth of tribal oral tradition.

The early representations of Kokopelli-like figures have no hump or phallus. These older figures are simple flute players who were probably used to draw spiritual power through the music of the flute. Many tribal people believe that music is innately spiritual and can build spiritual power for ceremony and healing. The simple flute players were probably carved to serve this type of function for the shaman's rituals.

As the people of the Southwest started cultivating maize and other crops, there emerged a new focus on the magic of fertility. Fertility magic was needed to help produce vigorous and abundant crops. But fertility magic was not limited to plants. There was also a need for more people to plant, care for, defend, and harvest the vital crops. To a hunter-gatherer, extra children were an additional burden that was difficult to bear. But to the farmer, extra children meant more land could be cultivated, protected, and more of a food surplus produced. So the work of fertility magic was extended to childbirth. With the rise of agriculture, pueblos formed and supported the growing population and the deities that served the interests of that increased population.

Kokopelli used the spirit power of his characteristic flute to serve the growing needs of fertility, just as Pan did in the Old World. Kokopelli was reputed to have brought a pack of seeds with him from the underworld or from his trading journeys to South America. Later depictions of Kokopelli earned him his symbolic erection that ensured the fertility of the people, and with it, the daughters and sons of the people to carry on the pueblo way of life.

Before the advent of the Katsina religion, Kokopelli was a main figure in the pantheon of the pueblo people. The shaman used petroglyph images of Kokopelli to bless the crops, and bring healthy children to the people of the tribe. The form of Kokopelli may have changed in light of local fertility tradition, taking on insect or other features, but his purpose was always the same.

Kokopelli-centered rituals were probably tied to the needs of the crops. Rituals were probably performed during planting, germination, flowering, and harvest. There were most likely fertility rituals for the collective benefit of the people. Additionally through shamanic intermediaries, appeals were made to Kokopelli on behalf of individuals who were unable to conceive. Fertility rituals are universal among tribal people, and Kokopelli was the most likely candidate for fulfilling those particular needs.

Hunters

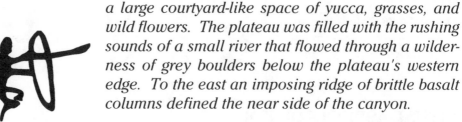

Craggy columns of volcanic rock encircled a flat green plateau leaving a large courtyard-like space of yucca, grasses, and wild flowers. The plateau was filled with the rushing sounds of a small river that flowed through a wilderness of grey boulders below the plateau's western edge. To the east an imposing ridge of brittle basalt columns defined the near side of the canyon.

Within the protected confines of the plateau a gallery of petroglyphs presented themselves in bold and colorful relief on the sides of the surrounding rock. Standing near one section of the gallery, a group of people focused their attention on the actions of a single old man.

The hunters, their faces solemn, stood just behind the shaman with their bows and quills of arrows. Snow Flint put the finishing touches of red paint on the hunt petroglyph. Wind Feather, his apprentice, took the stone cups of ocher and turquoise from her teacher. She stood back and surveyed Snow Flint's work. The wall now held the beautiful red and blue images of a hunter shooting arrows into the side of a running elk. Snow Flint sat down in front of the new images and motioned the hunters to do the same.

"You shall bind yourselves to the animals, the game and the spirits of this new land. You must begin the hunter's chant as I journey to the spirit world," intoned the shaman.

The hunters began to sing the familiar phrases of their chant, their voices filled with emotion. Snow Flint took a long drink from a small gourd canteen and closed his eyes.

Half a day later, the voices of the hunters were low and rough sounding. With a jolt, Snow Flint opened his eyes, looked at each of the hunters and put his hand out. The leader of the hunters placed his bow in the shaman's hand. His hands shaking with the power of the spirit, Snow Flint tapped the end of the bow on the new petroglyph hunt scene. The shaman than held the bow to the earth and mumbled in unintelligible spirit-talk before handing it back to the hunt leader. The next senior hunter handed his bow to Snow Flint, as did the rest of the hunters until all the bows had been blessed.

Watching the process Wind Feather could see the spiritual power jump from the glyph panel to the bow like embers from a fire. She wondered if she would ever be able to control as much power, or if she *would be able to command as much respect from the members of the tribe. Snow Flint exuded power and ability.*

The hunters, after leaving offerings of meat and arrow flight feathers on a small ledge near the new petroglyphs, gathered their belongings and returned to the pueblo where they would prepare for tomorrow's hunt.

"I hope we can have a feast tomorrow night, it has been too long," said Wind Feather, with hunger in her voice.

"Be patient! The hunters have made their call and our brothers, the elk and the deer, will see to our needs." admonished the shaman.

"You made the call. I saw the power of your ritual," replied Wind Feather as she collected the hammer tools and paint minerals.

"It is not my power. It is the power of the Spirit. I only seek it out and bring it here."

"I don't think that I will ever be able to gather as much power as you do," complained Wind Feather

With momentary anger the shaman turned to his apprentice. "Bring the hammer tools here. You can gather as much power as I but first you will need a rattle. You have asked me how a shaman makes the stone images to control the Spirit. Now is the time for you to learn. You will start with the rattle because it is an important tool of the shaman; it calls the Spirit, holds it and allows you to use it for your needs. In the future you can use the images left to us by our ancestors or you can make new ones if your heart is pure and you have listened to your teacher."

"I have been listening!"

"Yes. Now let me show you the right way to hold the tools and strike the stone," said Snow Flint as he placed Wind Feather's smooth fingers around the hammer.

PETROGLYPH OBJECTS

HORNED AND HEADDRESSED ANTHROPOMORPHS

Petroglyphs of horned anthropomorphs are common in the Upper Little Colorado region. These representations could depict actual headdresses worn during ceremonial activities, or they may represent spiritual encounters with supernatural beings during vision quests induced by physical deprivation, meditation or drug use.

Modern Hopi informants attribute the horned petroglyphs to members of the Two Horn Society of the Bow Clan (Grant 1978). Horns are equated with power, shamans' spirits or the shaman himself (Vastokas/Vastokas 1973, Grant 1978, et al).

It is sometimes difficult to distinguish between horned figures and anthropomorphic petroglyphs that include insect-like antennae. This is further complicated by glyphs that often illustrate elaborate headdresses.

Photos 28 and 29. Petroglyphs from north of Raven Site Ruins in east/central Arizona showing horned figures. Horns are associated with power, shaman's spirits or the shaman himself. The figure in Photo 29 also exhibits the rigid stance and three fingers and toes which are also associated with shamans and the pueblo creation myth.

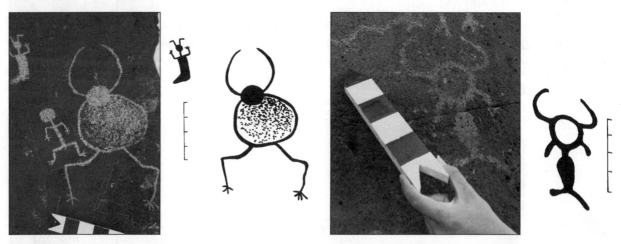

Photos 30 and 31. Horned petroglyph figures from north of Raven Site Ruins. The figures in these photos may illustrate horns or insect-like antennae.

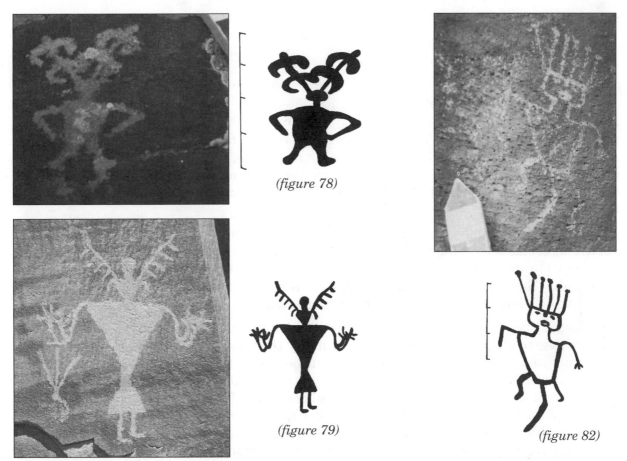

(figure 78)

(figure 79)

(figure 82)

Petroglyphs from east / central Arizona showing anthropomorphs with headdresses. The headdress (see photo with figure 78 above) has been interpreted by modern Hopi as a "corn" headdress.

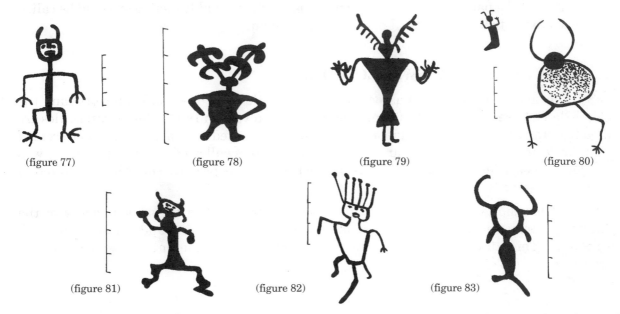

(figure 77)   (figure 78)   (figure 79)   (figure 80)

(figure 81)   (figure 82)   (figure 83)

Figures 77-83. Horned and headdressed petroglyphs from the Upper Little Colorado region of east / central Arizona.

RITUAL ASPECTS OF HORNED FIGURES

Horns represent power. The tribal people watched the deer, antelope and elk herds around them and saw that in the animal kingdom, the leader and most powerful members of the herd had horns. Horns were a natural headdress, a symbol of authority and strength.

It was common for a shaman to use a headdress with horns as part of ritual garb. In shamanic ritual and later kiva ceremonies, feathers, prayer-sticks and altar-boards were all implements of rituals and shrines. These sacred tools projected prayer skyward to the heavens and the spirit world. Horns, like the feathers of a headdress, established a connection between leaders and the spirit world. Like old Europeans believing their god conveyed his wishes through monarchs, the tribal people believed those in authority could receive visions directly from their gods.

Horned petroglyphs were often depictions of a shaman on the earthly plane. Unlike depictions of shamans in the spirit world where they needed no legs or solid body, a shaman in the physical world had legs and solid bodies. Horns have been a symbol of shamanic office worldwide. The completely articulated bodies of these petroglyphs coupled with the horns are symbolic of a spiritual leader, in most cases a shaman.

Other horned leaders could have been tribal chieftains or clan leaders. These leaders had a lesser degree of spiritual or ritual responsibility than a shaman, but had greater secular responsibilities. Depictions of these leaders could be used by the shaman to ritually strengthen those depicted. A tribal chieftain might also have been carved in stone upon his ascent to power. Petroglyphs marking the ascent of a leader could have acted to inform the spirit world so that the individual would receive the power and vision due him in his office. Likewise the shaman might have had his or her image carved in stone to mark an ascent to full shamanic status, thus securing spiritual power. In any case, a petroglyph depiction would allow the shaman to work with the spirit of the represented individual and to include him in needed rituals.

Many of these images are of specific deities, whose powers are symbolized by their horns. Such deities can be patrons of shamans or patrons of other tribal leaders who could be called upon to serve the tribe or the ritual needs of the shaman.

STICK/ARROW/SWORD SWALLOWERS

Stick or arrow swallowing is associated with the Hle'wekwe (Wood Fraternity) and the Ma'ke 'Hlan'nakwe (Great Fire Fraternity) of the Zuni (Stevenson 1902). These fraternities are called Nasotan at Hopi. After an elaborate ceremony that lasted several days had been created to influence the weather, sticks, arrows or swords were swallowed. This swallowing was considered to be a demonstration of shamanistic power. This practice sometimes resulted in death.

Several examples of stick/arrow swallowing can be found in the rock imagery of the Southwest. Sometimes these glyphs are interpreted as flute players and not arrow or stick swallowers. This difficulty is probably due to the limits of detail inherent to most petroglyphic depictions.

Photo 35. Petroglyph from south of Holbrook, Arizona showing an anthropomorph performing the stick / arrow swallowing ceremony. This petroglyph illustrates the confusion that is sometimes encountered identifying stick / arrow swallowers and flute players.

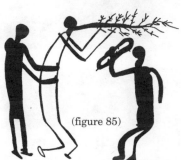

(figure 84)

Figure 84. Petroglyph near La Cieneguilla, New Mexico showing an anthropomorph with distinctive Kokopelli features including a humpback and erection who is either stick swallowing or playing a "branched" flute. (Slifer / Duffield 1994).

Figure 85. Stick swallower illustration painted on a Sikyatki pottery vessel. (Fewkes 1895).

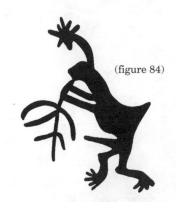

(figure 85)

Figure 86. Petroglyph from White Rock Canyon, New Mexico showing either a stick swallower with Kokopelli characteristics including an erection and humpback or Kokopelli playing a "branched" flute. (Slifer / Duffield 1994).

(figure 86)

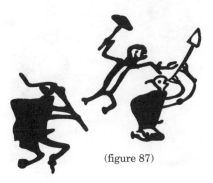

(figure 87)

Figure 87. Arrow swallower petroglyph from Bandelier National Monument, New Mexico. The anthropomorphs in this depiction have been interpreted as Kokopellis performing the arrow swallowing ceremony. (Rohn 1989 [Patterson 1992]).

(figure 88)

Figure 88. Petroglyph from Galisteo Dike (left) and Comanche Gap (right), New Mexico showing arrow swallowers. (Sims 1963 [Patterson 1992]).

Photo 36. Prehistoric ceramic bowl showing stick / sword swallowing. (White Mountain Archaeological Center Collections. St. Johns, Arizona).

Figure 89. Sword swallowers of Ma'ke 'Hlan'nakwe (Great Fire Fraternity). (Stevenson 1902).

Photo courtesy Bureau of American Ethnology

RITUAL ASPECTS OF STICK SWALLOWERS

Stick and sword swallowing is a worldwide phenomenon. In the east, it still survives as part of larger traditions, such as yoga, that put a premium on mastery of the body as a means of self-transcendence. Among shamanic peoples the meaning and purpose is very similar. By swallowing the stick, the shaman demonstrated a superhuman mastery of the body. This ability was believed to originate from the shaman's spiritual strength.

As a demonstration of shamanic power, these petroglyphs are overtly shamanic in nature. They were probably used to bring a shaman strength in ritual practice. The production of such a glyph may have been a mark of shamanic achievement that simultaneously created a tool of shamanic ritualism.

By setting themselves apart from the common person, the shaman maintained tribal belief in his spiritual authority. With such belief came the necessary acceptance of the shaman's power and the expectation of results from shamanic ritual. When ritual is supported by strong belief it is most effective.

The ritual of stick swallowing may have been a rite of initiation for an apprentice shaman. By publicly demonstrating their ability in such a straightforward public manner, they would remove all possible doubt as to their ability. Those who failed, or died, would be proven unready to meet the requirements of the shamanic office.

As the pueblo societies adopted the rituals of shamanism, the stick swallowing ritual was performed by select clans which used the inherent power of the ritual for their own purposes such as rainmaking among the Zuni. This practice still continues among tribal people in remote parts of the world, a ritual relic of a shamanic past.

BOW AND ARROW/WEAPONS

Petroglyphs depicting use of the bow and arrow are common in the Upper Little Colorado region and they have also been frequently recorded at most rock imagery sites throughout the Southwest.

The use of the bow and arrow is believed to have been introduced to the Southwest around the year A.D. 400 (Cordell 1984). This means that petroglyphs that illustrate the bow and arrow would have to have been created after A.D. 400 making it possible to at least relatively date them.

Petroglyphs illustrating the use of the bow and arrow usually include an anthropomorph holding the bow with the arrow at the ready and an unsuspecting quadruped as the target. It would appear that these panels are recording an actual hunt. This may well be the case. However, current research into the nature of these and other petroglyph panels is revealing that in many cases these hunt scenes may be illustrating hunts that occurred on a spiritual level rather than a physical level. These depictions may also have been created to draw power to the weapons used, ensure success of the hunt to the hunter and to honor the spirit of the game animals.

Bow and arrow illustrations are not uncommon as ceramic depictions. Mimbres bowls often illustrate not only hunting scenes where the bow and arrow is employed, but also depictions of hunters gambling for arrows.

Photo 37. Petroglyph from south of Holbrook, Arizona showing an anthropomorph with bow and arrow facing a quadruped.

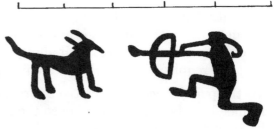

Photo 38. Petroglyph from south of Holbrook, Arizona showing an anthropomorph with bow and arrow and quadruped. Notice the missing rock area where the scale is resting. This section of petroglyph panel was stolen by looters.

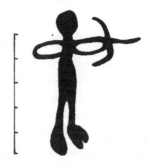

Photo 39. Petroglyph from south of Holbrook, Arizona showing a standing anthropomorph with bow and arrow. Bow and arrow depictions can be relatively dated as post-A.D. 400.

Photo 40. *Petroglyph from south of Holbrook, Arizona showing anthropomorph with a bow and arrow at the ready. Notice the two bullet holes just below the petroglyph. Bullet hole vandalism is very common to petroglyph areas with little or no site stewardship.*

Photo 41. *Petroglyph from south of Holbrook, Arizona. This depiction includes the kneeling archer and another figure kneeling just behind. This could be an attempt at perspective, or this panel may be depicting a father and son. Notice the line from the arrow to the quadruped.*

(figure 90)

(figure 91)

Figure 90. *Bow and hourglass petroglyphs, Largo Canyon drainage. (Schaafsma 1980).*

Figure 91. *Mimbres bowl dating from A.D. 950 to A.D. 1150 illustrating a bear hunter using a bow and arrow. (LeBlanc 1983).*

Figure 92. *Mimbres bowl dating from A.D. 950 to A.D. 1150 showing hunters gambling for arrows. The small dots on the corners of the gaming blanket are representations of broken and ground ceramic sherds that were used to keep score. The figure at the right holds a small cup which was used to throw the dice. These dice were also made from pieces of broken ceramic vessels. (Brody 1977).*

(figure 92)

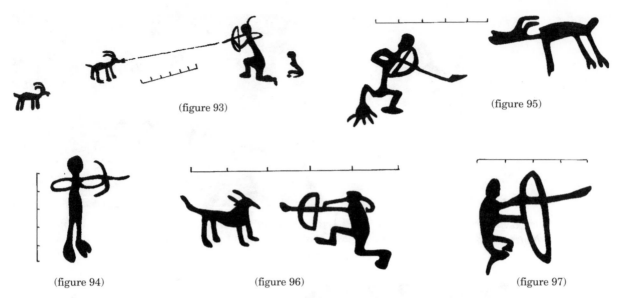

(figure 93)

(figure 95)

(figure 94)

(figure 96)

(figure 97)

Figures 93-97. Hunters and bow and arrow petroglyphs from the Upper Little Colorado region. Creating the magic of the hunt helped ensure success by empowering the weapons used and by honoring the game animals to be hunted.

RITUAL ASPECTS OF WEAPONS

Most hunt scenes are not the records of specific events. Instead they empowered components of shamanic hunt rituals. These rituals are among the oldest and most commonly found in pictographs and petroglyphs. Hunt rituals used the principles of sympathetic magic to empower the hunter, control the game and secure the success of the hunt. Weapons were depicted in hunt petroglyphs to empower the weapons, ensuring flawless operation to kill the prey. Some petroglyphs show a line connecting the weapon to the prey. These lines were instructive to the spirit of the weapon. Weapons could be instructed because, according to animists, they had a powerful spiritual element. It was obvious that weapons had physical power and such power would have its naturally corresponding spiritual component. Weapons demonstrated their spiritual power by opening the doorway to the spirit world via death.

Petroglyph depictions of weapons were believed to act directly on the prey by ritually instructing game on the manner of its demise. Hunt rituals honored the prey and secured permission of the prey's spirit to take the body. This permission prevented the quarry's spirit from taking vengeance on the living and also guided the spirit to the cycle of rebirth. The rebirth of prey maintained an abundance of game that could be hunted again and again.

Hunt magic also increased the power and skill of the hunter. Weapon petroglyphs could have been used to attune the spirit of the hunter with the spirit of the weapon. The magic of ritual bonded the hunter to his weapon making the weapon an extension of the hunter.

Weapons were only one part of the interacting beings, tools, and energies of the hunter's craft. Through the magic of ritual, the shaman carefully crafted a specific spiritual reality, that of a successful hunt. Because the physical was tied to the spiritual, the physical reality of the hunt would unfold along the preexisting lines of the spiritual reality.

RATTLES AND SYMBOLS OF EMERGENCE LEVELS

A common glyph found in the Upper Little Colorado River area is a circle or a linear series of circles with a line through the center. The circle or circles are sometimes pecked in outline only or are filled in completely. A single circle with the line through the center is believed to represent the atlatl, a prehistoric weapon that predates the bow and arrow.

A circle or multiple circles with the intersecting line often is an illustration of a rattle and/or the idea of the several levels of emergence that were prevalent in prehistoric mythology. Rattles embody a symbolic meaning beyond their simple representation as a physical object. Rattles were used in curing ceremonies and were probably employed in a wide range of ceremonial functions.

Very often these petroglyphs of rattles depict a series of four circles with the intersecting line which represents the underworlds and this fourth world of the present. Also built into this representation is the idea that the four discs of the rattle will bring the rains from the four directions.

"The four discs of the gourd represent the four underworlds and are called *na'liyum ki'hu naach'vee,* four houses superincumbent. Each disc is double; i.e., two discs are sewed together. They are held in place on the rod with a thong of deerskin. At the back of the discs is attached a slender crook with shells...as a rattle...This ...is to typify the roar and commotion of the waters at the early sipapu. Between this crook and the discs is a *hewakinpi* (tumo'ala is the pod they grow on), on an eagle wing feather. These...are to hook the clouds this way from all directions." (Stephen 1936).

Several petroglyphs from the Upper Little Colorado region depict anthropomorphs holding two rattles, one in each hand. Usually each rattle is shown with four discs. These petroglyphs have been discovered in various locations and in most instances the rattles held by anthropomorphs have the four discs, rarely two or three.

Near Puerco Ruin in the Petrified Forest National Monument is a petroglyph depicting an anthropomorph holding two rattles. One of the rattles has the standard four discs, and the other has only two.

Representations of circles with the intersecting line without the inclusion of the anthropomorph are a very common petroglyph and almost any number of circles in a row can be demonstrated. One circle with the intersecting line is believed to represent the atlatl, multiple circles with the intersecting line are believed to represent rattles or the idea of different levels of emergence or existence. Multiple circles with the intersecting line that are not being held in the hand of an anthropomorph are probably representing the idea of emergence/level of existence rather than the physical object of the rattle. One interesting example discovered south of Holbrook shows an anthropomorph in the "prayer" stance, with the four circles superimposed within his stick figure body. These four circles probably display the idea of emergence or levels of existence.

Photo 42. Petroglyph south of Holbrook, Arizona showing an anthropomorph holding two rattles each with the four discs.

Photo 43. Petroglyph south of Holbrook, Arizona showing anthropomorph holding two rattles, each with four discs.

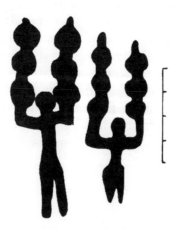

Photo 44. Petroglyph south of Holbrook, Arizona showing a pair of anthropomorphs holding two rattles each. This glyph displays only three discs on each rattle instead of the usual four.

Figure 98. Petroglyph near Puerco Ruins, Petrified Forest National Monument showing an anthropomorph holding two rattles, one with the standard four discs and the other with only two (Ritter and Ritter 1973).

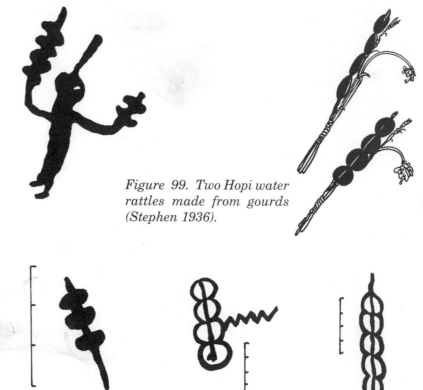

Figure 99. Two Hopi water rattles made from gourds (Stephen 1936).

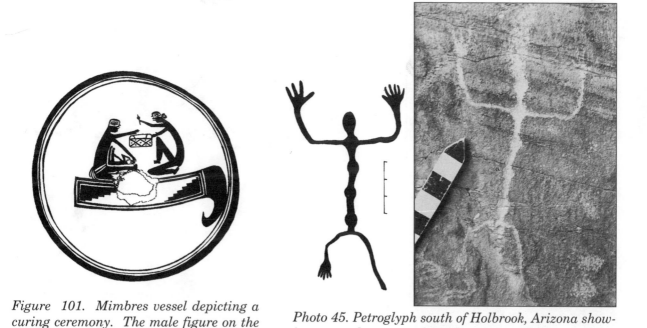

Figure 100. Petroglyphs from the Upper Little Colorado River area showing from two to five outlined circles with the intersecting line. These probably represent levels of emergence or existence.

Figure 101. Mimbres vessel depicting a curing ceremony. The male figure on the right is holding a small single disc rattle. (Brody 1977).

Photo 45. Petroglyph south of Holbrook, Arizona showing an anthropomorph in the "prayer/blessing" stance with the four circles superimposed over his stick figure.

Figure 102. Mimbres bowl dating between A.D. 950 and A.D. 1150 depicting emergence. The anthropomorph in the center of the bowl is holding a symbol with seven levels which represent the seven levels of existence in pueblo mythology. This symbol is crowned with a plumed serpent's head (Fewkes 1923).

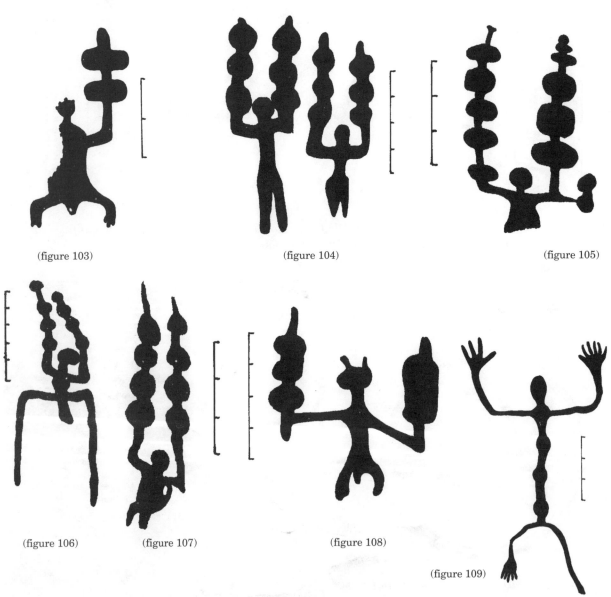

(figure 103)   (figure 104)   (figure 105)

(figure 106)   (figure 107)   (figure 108)

(figure 109)

Figures 103-109. Petroglyphs from the Upper Little Colorado region showing anthropomorphs holding rattles and possible rattles/levels of emergence or existence.

RITUAL ASPECTS OF RATTLES AND EMERGENCE GLYPHS

Rattles were an important shamanic tool often used in healing rituals. The sound of the rattle, like the rhythm of drums and chanting, helped bring about the spirit trance of the shaman. From the spirit trance, the shaman could enter the supernatural world and correct any disharmony of spirit that animists believed to be the cause of illness.

The sound of the rattle was also used to draw upon particular spiritual energies; in most cases, healing energies. Each tribal culture and shamanic tradition assigned different values to the form and color of the rattle which determined the spiritual energy the rattle would conduct for shamanic use. The number of rattle heads may have determined the specific powers or the intensity of those powers conducted. The four gourd rattle can represent the power of the four winds or the power from each of the four worlds that have existed in the mythology of the pueblo peoples. Petroglyph representations were not limited by the practical limitations of physical rattles, so the shaman could carve them with as many heads as needed to draw upon whatever powers desired.

Petroglyph depictions of rattles could be used in ways that were not possible for their physical counterparts. Petroglyph healing symbols could be used to heal at a distance in times of war or heal large groups of people during times of widespread illness. One can easily imagine the shaman using a petroglyph shrine in an effort to heal his stricken tribe during an outbreak of smallpox. The rattle symbol is not always a rattle. In some cases what appears to be a rattle was a depiction of linear emergence levels. Emergence refers to the mythological exodus of the tribes from the underworld that housed them before the existence of this physical world. This time of emergence was a creation event, thus filled with the transformational power of creation. Petroglyph depictions of emergence likewise produced creation power useful in a broad range of ritual. Creation power could be used in rituals of birth, animal rebirth, fertility, agriculture and others.

Emergence levels can also be symbolic of the personal emergence or transition of the person from one level of being to the next. Many tribal people believed that people went through distinct stages of personal development (birth, adulthood, parenthood, wisdom etc.) and that these transitions could be best facilitated through the harmonizing influence of ritual.

ANTHROPOMORPHS WITH STAFFS

Petroglyphs illustrating anthropomorphs holding staffs or crooks are not uncommon throughout the Southwest. These staffs have been interpreted as religious paraphernalia, i.e., prayer-sticks, wands, fertility symbols and rain-bringing devices.

The crook resembles the "shepherd's staff" used by herdsmen throughout the world. However, most prehistoric depictions throughout the Southwest illustrate this object much smaller and it may be a bent reed which was used in conjunction with other rain-bringing paraphernalia (Sims 1949). The reed or cane is also associated with the emergence myth. It was through the use of a cane or reed that the people climbed up into the fourth world. Crooks are also associated with fertility and long life (Parsons 1985, Cole 1989 [Patterson 1992]).

Another interpretation of the crook is that it is a replica of an ancient weapon (probably the atlatl) which was later used to instill power in warriors. "These crooks, or gnelas, have been called warrior prayer sticks, and are symbols of ancient weapons. In many folk tales it is stated that the warriors overcame their foes by the use of gnelas which would indicate that they had something to do with ancient war implements. Their association with arrows on the Antelope altars (Hopi) adds weight to this conclusion." (Fewkes 1914-1924).

Staffs and crooks are a very common addition to depictions found on Mimbres ceramics. The two forms seem very distinct. The bent reed crook is usually carried by burden bearers and the phallic staff is often included with depictions of various zoomorphic forms and other fertility symbols.

Photos 46 and 47. Petroglyphs from the Upper Little Colorado area showing anthropomorphs with crooks. These may have been bent reeds used as religious paraphernalia to bring rain.

Figure 110. Hopi curved stick used in ceremonies identified as a replica of an ancient weapon, probably the atlatl. This emblem is associated with warriors. (Fewkes 1914-1924).

Figures 111, 112 and 113. Mimbres Black-on-white bowls dating between A.D. 950 and A.D. 1150 showing crooks. Crooks are often shown held by burden bearers. Figure 113 illustrates what is probably the most graphic known depiction of Kokopelli. (Brody 1977).

Figures 114, 115, and 116 (left to right). Staffs other than crooks are very commonly depicted on Mimbres ceramics, and are less frequently encountered on the rock art of the Southwest. These staffs probably have fertility significance and they are often shown with various animals. Both symbols representing the male and female are included at the head of the staff. The female element is the Maltese cross component beneath the phallic head (LeBlanc 1983 and Brody 1983).

Figure 117. Wooden staffs from caves in New Mexico. These rare artifacts are probably the staffs which are so abundantly depicted on Mimbres ceramics (LeBlanc 1983).

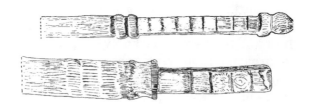

RITUAL ASPECTS OF STAFFS

The staff was most likely a signet of station that had its origin as a weapon. The oldest traditional weapons were the spear, club, pole-staff and atlatl, all of which can look alike in glyphic depictions. In a society of hunters and warriors, weapons were potent tools of authority. The leaders in such societies would often hold special weapons. In this way, the simple staff made the transition from a weapon to a symbol of authority. The staff played the same role as the scepter, which was originally a mace-like weapon that became a symbol of a king's power in the European tradition.

If the staff was portrayed in a hunt or war scene, it was probably being used as one of the traditional weapons and was part of the hunt magic that motivated the creation of these panels. However, there are few depictions of the staff in hunt panels, leading to the assumption that they were used in other forms of ritual.

The petroglyph depictions of beings with staffs is less concerned with the specific meaning of the staff than it is with the meaning of the whole being. The staff helped mark or identify the character being portrayed and the role they served in the shaman's ritual. The staff may have represented fertility or power in warfare, but the staff was not the source of this power. The source was the being who held the staff.

If the staff represented fertility to the tribe, it would symbolize the fertility power of the possessor. The petroglyph rendering of this same individual would, according to the rules of sympathetic magic, be empowered with the spirit of fertility. Such individuals, be they actual leaders of the tribe or mythic characters, could have their particular power directed by the shamanic rituals that required this type of petroglyph representation.

NETS/FENCES

Designs that resemble nets or fences are not uncommon in the rock imagery of the Upper Little Colorado region. When these appear in isolation with no other associated glyphs they are often classified in the murky petroglyph category of "geometric". Many of these meshed patterns are lightly scratched into the desert patina rather than deeply pecked. This light scratching technique often raises suspicion as to whether these depictions are in fact contemporaneous with other deeply pecked rock art on the same stone panel, or whether they were created later — possibly even by modern "artists".

One net or fence petroglyph discovered east of Raven Site Ruins in east/central Arizona illustrates two anthropomorphs (see photo 48). In the foreground and behind a net or fence is a figure identified as a male. The smaller figure to the left may represent a female (there appears to be hair whorls illustrated on either side of the head.) Both the net and the anthropomorphs are pecked into the stone surface. The net was pecked somewhat more lightly than the anthropomorphs, but both elements appear to have been created at the same time.

This petroglyph is located at a prehistoric shrine site. Many petroglyph sites are associated with shrines, i.e., places of offering and prayer. Rabbit nets similar to this petroglyph depiction have been discovered in dry caves very near this panel. These nets were often made from human hair and they are remarkably long and wide. The nets were utilized by stretching them across an area and then driving the rabbits into them. These rabbit drives would often involve whole communities, men, women and children. The rabbits were then dispatched by means of a throwing stick which is very similar to the aboriginal boomerang, except not so sharply curved.

Photo 48. *Petroglyph from east of Raven Site Ruins, Arizona showing two anthropomorphs one male and one female behind a net or fence. Rabbit nets which were often made from human hair have been discovered in dry caves very near this depiction.*

Figure 118. *Mimbres Black-on-white bowl, A.D. 950 to A.D. 1150 illustrating a rabbit hunt. This depiction is complete with hunters, rabbits, throwing sticks, and the rabbit net. The net shown on this bowl shares the meshed diamond pattern of the petroglyph in Photo 48. (Brody 1977).*

RITUAL ASPECTS OF NETS AND FENCES

The petroglyph net was often a component of hunt magic. The net, like the spear, or the bow was a tool for hunting, but was primarily used for small game. Small game is much less common in petroglyph depictions than the larger more dramatic prey. The net is more significant as a tool of hunting than the game it was used to capture. The portrayal strengthened the net and possibly empowered it to attract small game.

A second purpose of the net petroglyph was to control or limit a preexisting image. The net was produced at a later date to capture the power of a petroglyph that may have been produced by an earlier people. Glyphs that predate the traditions or mythic school of a particular shaman may have been perceived as dangerous, requiring a control mechanism. As such, a net image may only have been employed with particular petroglyphs and by the shamans of particular cultures.

The net may also have been produced with the image it seems to capture. This would serve to preemptively control a known image (possibly an evil being) which would otherwise pose an active threat to the tribe. The shaman would produced a petroglyph of the threatening being captured and controlled by the symbolic net. So regulated, the power of the captured image could be safely used in ritual activity.

Figure 119. Mimbres Black-on-white bowl A.D. 950 to A.D. 1150 showing a man in front of a fence or rabbit net. Notice the diamond pattern of the net. (Brody 1977 [McSherry Site, Gila Drainage. ASM Collection]).

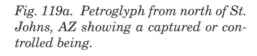

Fig. 119a. Petroglyph from north of St. Johns, AZ showing a captured or controlled being.

The Dead

The tribe's new land embraced the people. The construction of the pueblo on the foundations of an ancestral settlement was going well and the land proved rich in the berries, roots, and plants the people needed. When the hunting party sent members back over the course of five days with more and more game, the tribe rejoiced. Skillfully, the people prepared and preserved enough meat for weeks and still had enough for the feast. The feast would be a celebration of their migration's end, of establishing their home and of the successful hunt. The people were weary from their long trek. The feast would fill them, give their bodies new strength and refresh their spirits.

Snow Flint could see the glowing fires of the pueblo and hear the distant sounds of merriment as he stood next to the death shrine. It had been hard climbing to the high plateau and then on up to the shrine. His legs hurt and the pains in his chest were getting worse.

Snow Flint was happy that Wind Feather was proving to be such a capable apprentice. He had made the young woman stay behind at the celebration. It was important for a young shaman to sustain a personal life and to maintain a close connection to the tribe by being with them in times of joy, ritual, and sorrow.

Snow Flint started a small fire. In the flames he could see the grim face of the death deity and the impaled figure of a dying warrior. During the course of the migration, six people had died, and now that the tribe had found a place to settle, their spirits had to be guided to their rightful place in the underworld. The dead were always unwilling to leave the land of the living and could bring illness and misfortune if allowed to remain. Reluctantly, he prepared himself for a ritual that was always difficult.

The shaman looked into the fire and let himself fall into the familiar trance. He called upon the centipede to guide any spirits to the underworld that might still be following the people. He asked the deity of death to admit the dead and prepare them for their new existence. The faces of the newly departed swam before him, pleading to stay. With a stern voice he sent them forth with the centipede. His mind swam with images of spirits descending into the bright portal of the underworld.

With the tribe safe from the influences of wandering spirits, Snow Flint could relax and review the rituals for the next day. But he could not focus his mind. He was haunted by a spirit that remained in the world of the living, one he had been reluctant to send away. He lay back under a thick pelt, feeling older than ever before and remembered the face of his dead wife.

DEATH AND SPIRITS

SPIRITUAL TRANSITION, LEVEL CHANGES, DEATH

Figure 120 is a Mimbres Classic Black-on-white bowl that has been rediscovered after having been hidden from academia in a private collection for several decades. This fantastic bowl was looted early in the 1960's. It was sold and resold several times over the next several decades and its whereabouts today is unknown. A small photograph of the vessel came into my hands in the early 1980's and this photograph remained in my files for several years. While assembling this study several petroglyphs were discovered that share much of the symbolism displayed on this bowl.

The vessel presents an anthropomorph holding a large centipede in his right hand. He is wearing an elaborate headdress. His body has been pierced by a large arrow. His midsection displays a spiral and his internal organs including his genitals appear to be hanging loose and lying on the ground. His legs are turned upwards as is his left hand. This representation has a wealth of information that can support the interpretation of many important petroglyphs in the Upper Little Colorado River region. The anthropomorph has been pierced by an arrow and he is dying. His internal organs, his life breath, his whirlwind is escaping. "...myth explains that a stranger came among the people, when a great whirlwind blew all the vegetation from the surface of the earth and all the water from its courses. With a flint he caught these symbols upon a rock, the etching of which is now in Keam's Canyon....He told them he was the keeper of the breath. The whirlwind and the air which men breathe come from this keeper's mouth." (Mallery 1893 [Patterson 1992]).

The above legend greatly resembles the story of creation in Genesis when God created man and breathed into his nostrils the breath of life.

The centipede represents the transition from the world of the living to the world of the dead. The centipede can be regarded as a ladder from which to ascend or descend from one level of existence to another. Because of this association with the dead, modern Hopi and Zuni will not even discuss this symbol.

The elaborate headdress is similar to depictions discovered on kiva murals from Pottery Mound, New Mexico and is undoubtedly ritualistic (Brody 1991, plate 16). The position of this anthropomorph's arms and legs is revealing. The legs and arms are turned upwards. He is entering the realm of the spirits. Legs are not necessary in the spirit world and they are often depicted turned upwards or one up and one down or even absent during transitional travel from one level of existence to another. A depiction of the spiral or the vortex identical to the life/breath whirlwind is often included with anthropomorphs shown in this transitional state. The upturned arms could represent prayer or blessing. Anthropomorphs with normal (living) leg stances and upturned arms are among the most common anthropomorphic images that are found in the rock art depictions.

Most rock art researchers agree that the upturned arms depict "prayer". I usually include "blessing" along with the idea of "prayer" or the "praying stance". Prayer and blessings are very similar concepts.

Figure 120. Mimbres Classic Black-on-white bowl dating between A.D. 950 to A.D. 1150. Dying anthropomorph holding centipede. His whirlwind or life breath is escaping. The legs are shown splayed upwards, needless in the spirit world. The centipede represents the underworld or ladder to ascend/descend to another level of existence/emergence.

Photo 49. Petroglyph from north of St. Johns, Arizona showing an almost identical depiction as the vessel in figure 120. Compare the position of the arms and legs, the arrow and internal organs, and the headdress. This glyph probably represents death and spiritual transition.

Photo 50. Petroglyph from north of St. Johns, Arizona showing anthropomorphs. The figure on the left has the "prayer/blessing" raised arm stance and an extension coming down and out of his body similar to the "whirlwind/life breath" depiction. The figure next to it displays the legs upward transitional state from one level of existence/emergence to another.

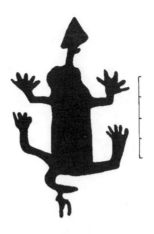

Photo 51. *Petroglyph from north of St. Johns, Arizona showing an anthropomorph with several common symbolic elements similar to Figure 120. The arms and legs are splayed upwards, there is an extension protruding out and down from his body analogous to the "whirlwind/life breath" spiral, and there is a representation of an arrow coming out of his head.*

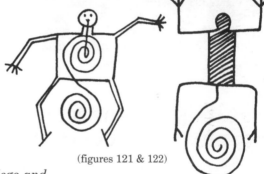

Figures 121 and 122. *Petroglyphs from Hopi Mesa, Arizona showing anthropomorphs with the "whirlwind/life breath" spiral. (Patterson 1992).*

(figures 121 & 122)

Figure 123. *Anthropomorph showing splayed upward legs and arms, "whirlwind/life breath spiral", protrusion from lower body, and the gnashing teeth death imagery. This depiction shares many common symbolic elements with the Mimbres bowl shown in Figure 120. (Awatovi room 529, Smith 1952 [Cole 1992]).*

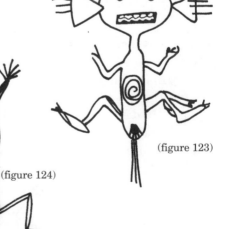

Figure 124. *Petroglyph from the Zuni Reservation, Arizona showing an anthropomorph with legs and arms splayed upwards and two "whirlwind/life breath" spirals emanating downwards (Young 1988).*

(figure 124)

(figure 123)

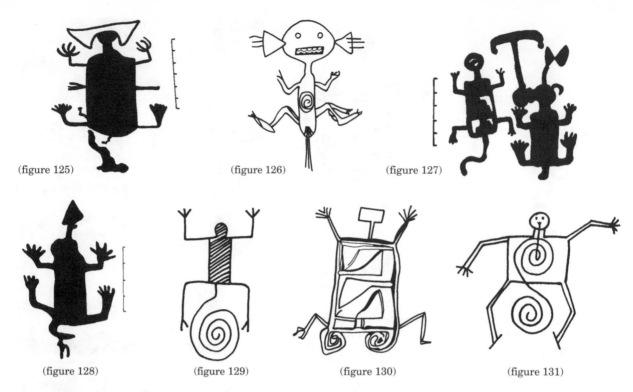

(figure 125) (figure 126) (figure 127)

(figure 128) (figure 129) (figure 130) (figure 131)

Figures 125-131. Petroglyphs and kiva murals showing common symbolic elements to the Mimbres bowl in figure 120. Death and transition to the spiritual realm is probably the theme of these depictions (Young 1988, Smith 1952, Patterson 1992).

RITUAL ASPECTS OF SPIRITUAL TRANSITION
AND DEATH PETROGLYPHS

The death-transition figures seen in petroglyphs and Mimbres vessels are similar in function to some components of hunt magic. The key components of hunt magic were maintaining the ability to kill the quarry and continuing the cycle of animal rebirth, while preventing animal spirit revenge. It is this danger of spirit revenge, as it applies to people, that motivated the production of death-transition petroglyphs.

Death-transition figures were directly concerned with the killing of people in times of conflict and war. The shaman would use these images to ensure that the victims of conflict would be conveyed to the spirit world. If victims were not sent to the spirit world, there existed the very disturbing possibility of spirit revenge. Hunt magic ensured that animals did not take revenge though they were less prone to that vice than humans. To the animist, the wild creatures had an innate nobility. They were more connected to the spiritual realms than people and did not readily display the need for revenge that was common to the people. Death-transition figures protected the living from the dangers of human nature.

The petroglyphs show the death of victims with a piercing arrow or disembowelment. The arrow depiction acted to both strengthen the power of the warrior and weaken the spiritual power of the victim. The depicted loss of internal organs also weakened the victim while sealing his death. The Mimbres depiction of detached genitalia strips the victim of his masculine/warrior power. Both spiral and internal organs can represent the loss of spirit from the body.

Once the spirit had been separated from the body it had to be guided to the spirit world. Otherwise the spirit would wander the physical world of the living bringing vengeance and harm. The "legs turned up stance" is a classic representation of a being entering the spirit world. This type of petroglyph depiction was a passive means of encouraging the victim's transition to the spirit world. The Mimbres artist (see Figure 120) went a step further, showing the victim holding a centipede. The centipede was an active guide to the spirit world, further ensuring the victim was removed from the world of the warrior.

Once the victim was safely sent to the spirit world, he was embraced by the animistic cosmos and reborn into the spirit world. Unlike prey animals, the shaman did not perform rituals to guide people to be reborn in the world of the living.

SPIRITS, GHOSTS, AND SPIRIT HELPERS

Petroglyphs that represent spirits, ghosts or spirit helpers appear as basically anthropomorphic representations but have distinctive characteristics. These figures are usually full-bodied, often including within the body design patterns such as diamonds, dots, vertical stripes or other intersecting lines. Many times these internal body designs resemble the rib cage or other skeletal depictions. They may also represent robes worn by the shaman.

Often the shape of the body is large at the shoulders and tapers to the feet, if feet are included. The feet or the entire lower body may be absent giving the figure a floating effect. Feet are not necessary in the spiritual plain. Thin horns or antennae are very common. The arms of these figures are usually flowing or wavy and very often a circular object is held in hand. The head of these figures is often almost skull-like with large hollow eyes and a rounded open mouth.

It is difficult to obtain any information about these ghost-like figures from modern Native American informants. Modern Native Americans have so many taboos about the dead that they will rarely discuss any figure that represents a ghost or spirit.

These figures may have been created during vision quests that were induced by intense prayer/meditation, physical deprivation, and/or the use of hallucinogenic drugs such as peyote or datura.

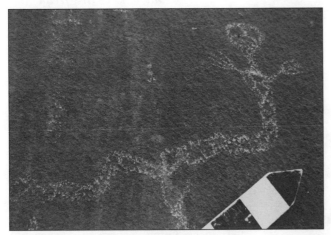
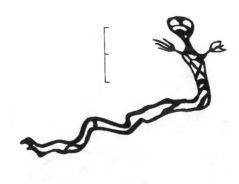

Photo 52. Spirit or ghost petroglyph from south of Holbrook, Arizona. This figure exhibits the skull-like head and a flowing, almost bodiless, form.

Photo 53. Petroglyph from south of Holbrook showing spirit or spirit helper. Horns or antennae are common, as are small or absent feet, and wavy arms. The head is often depicted with skull-like qualities.

Photo 54. Spirit or ghost petroglyph from north of St. Johns, Arizona.

Photo 55. Petroglyph panel from south of Holbrook, Arizona showing several spirits or spirit helpers. These figures are commonly found in groups. Bodies are often patterned and objects are frequently held in the hands.

Photo 56. Spirit or spirit helper petroglyph panel from south of Holbrook, Arizona with three figures. Often the body will taper into thin air. Feet will be absent or very small.

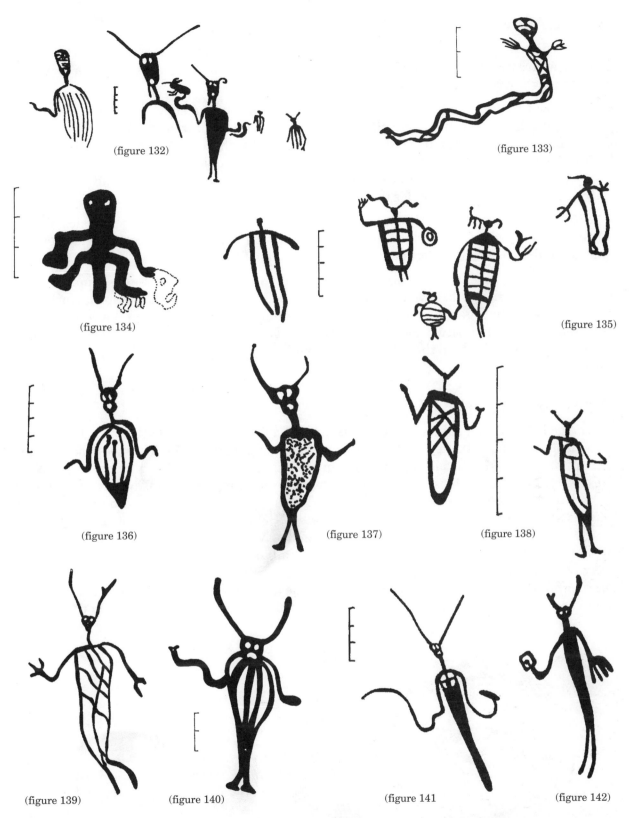

(figure 132)

(figure 133)

(figure 134)

(figure 135)

(figure 136)

(figure 137)

(figure 138)

(figure 139)

(figure 140)

(figure 141)

(figure 142)

Figures 132-142. Spirits, ghosts or spirit helpers from the Upper Little Colorado River region in east / central Arizona.

RITUAL ASPECTS OF SPIRITS

Spirit figures tended to have an unearthly quality about them. There is a good reason for this. These are figures of the spirit world. Spirits were often shown floating across a rock wall or suspended above a stone shrine.

The spirit figure may have been a familiar, or helper, of the shaman. When a shaman traveled into the spirit world, contacts were made and skills acquired to demand the services of spirit beings. Some shaman would create petroglyphs of these beings to establish a greater degree of personal control over them. In this way the shaman could call upon the beings in ritual as opposed to having to make an exhausting spirit journey. Shamans may have passed on control of the depicted spirit beings to their apprentices when they relinquished their practice.

Spirit figures may also have represented beings that were not native to the physical world, only entering it to do the bidding of the shaman. This would explain the common lack of legs and the fluid, non-corporeal form of the arms and body of these figures.

Lastly, spirit figures can be representations of the shaman. In the course of shamanic spirit travels, the shaman was believed to leave his body behind, journeying to the spirit world as a shamanic spirit. In this non-physical form, the shaman could travel behind the veil, visit the dead and adjust the spiritual mechanisms that drove the physical world. These depictions would sympathetically help the shaman leave behind the body and glide through the land of spirit.

DEATH, GOD OF DEATH, MAASAW

The god of death, or "Maasaw", or "Masauwu" originates in Hopi mythology. This figure often displays round hollow eyes and mouth and has a bulging forehead. The mouth sometimes appears as skull-like, that is, square with gnashing teeth. The bulging forehead is also a representation of the fleshless head. Several petroglyph examples of Maasaw have been found in the Upper Little Colorado region. The fleshless head with triangular nose and gnashing teeth as a representation of death was also used by Salado and Mimbres potters on ceramic depictions as early as A.D. 950. The "Janus Face" has been observed on the Jornada Style art (Schaafsma/Schaafsma 1974). This Janus face is similar to depictions from Mesoamerica and they are often associated with stories of death and rebirth. Petroglyphs illustrate the idea of death (other than the god Maasaw) by depicting the anthropomorph upside down or headless and in some cases underneath a horizontal line or surface level which represents the earth.

Figure 143. Mimbres ceramic bowl dating from A.D. 950 to A.D. 1150 with two figures (possibly the Warrior Twins) which display the fleshless triangular nose and gnashing teeth of the Jornada Style (Moulard 1984).

Headless figures are also sometimes interpreted as representing a "lesser god" or the evil twin brother of the Creator God. Often this figure will not be truly headless, but the head will be represented as partially incomplete or flattened. Good contextual representations of this idea can be found all along the Colorado River on the border between Arizona and California in the form of intaglios or giant geoglyphs (glyphs created on the surface of the ground). Both gods are represented and one (the evil twin brother) is shown with less cranial area (Boma Johnson personal communique).

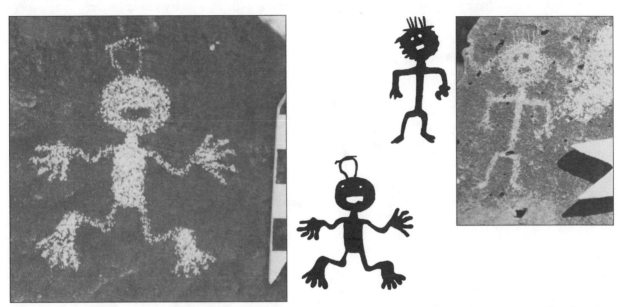

Photos 57 and 58. Petroglyphs from north of Raven Site Ruins in east / central Arizona possibly showing Maasaw figures. The depiction in photo includes exaggerated hands and feet.

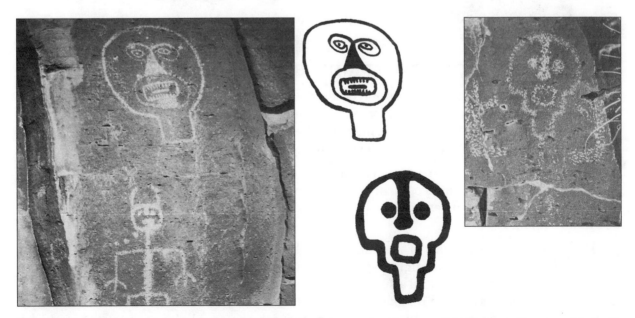

Photos 59 and 60. Petroglyphs from west of Eagar, Arizona showing possible Maasaw figures with skull-like qualities — including a fleshless triangular nose and gnashing teeth. These petroglyphs have similar characteristics to Jornada Style art found on both Salado and Mimbres ceramics.

Figure 144. Petroglyph from Willow Springs, Arizona showing the god of death in profile, illustrating the bulging forehead (Malotki/Lomat-uway'ma 1987).

Figure 145. Boundary stone between Shunopovi and Oraibi (Hopi lands) in the figure of Masauwu (Maasaw). (Stephen 1936 [Patterson 1992]).

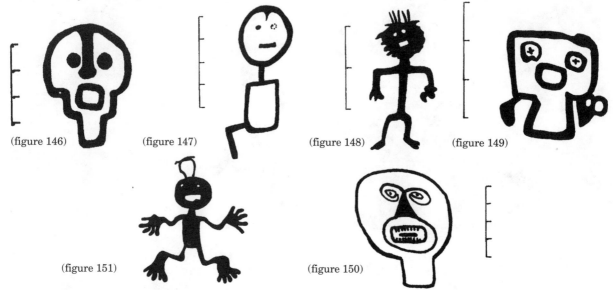

(figure 146)   (figure 147)   (figure 148)   (figure 149)

(figure 151)   (figure 150)

Figure 146-151. God of Death/Maasaw petroglyphs from the Upper Little Colorado River areas of east/central Arizona.

RITUAL ASPECTS OF DEATH FIGURES

As there were the Great Mothers and other gods of life, so too there had to be a god of death. The symmetry of the animistic world view demanded an embodiment of death, as there were deities of life existing in the world of spirit that balanced the world of flesh. The god of death was necessary to the cycle of life. Death was a necessary tool of the hunt, of conflict and of war.

The figure of the death god is usually well-defined. Petroglyphic depictions often have large hands and feet as well as a recognizable head. These figures denoted a particular being, not a general class. The god of death was a powerful and important being who had to be dealt with as an individual.

Death was an integral part of the hunt. It marked success and guided the spirit of the prey into the underworld so that it might enter the cycle of rebirth. The shaman appealed to death to ensure this cycle of rebirth and a successful hunt. Death could be ritually compelled to wield his power, that is, to kill — to remove specific enemies or to empower warriors in time of war. Because the god of death had power over death, the shaman could also seek to stay his hand. For the sake of healing the shaman would be forced to deal directly with death. Rituals built around the power of the death deity may have been one of the shaman's most important tools.

Mother Moon

Wind Feather liked the plateau of shrines. The gallery of petroglyphs spoke to her of the past, the power of the present and reassured her about the future. The future was what she and her teacher were concerned with today. Snow Flint was between a sheer rock wall and a mass of sagebrush. "Here it is," said the shaman from behind the tangle of branches. "I thought I saw her back here. We'll have to cut this brush away." Between the branches, Wind Feather could see the mineral-stained image of the crescent moon.

Wind Feather cut away the brush from the wall and when her work was finished, she looked around at the surrounding shrines. The moon image, like several other shrines they had cleared, enjoyed the open sunlight for the first time since their abandonment by the ancestors. With the tribe settled in this ancient land, old paths were being reworn, fields planted, and the shrines maintained and used again. The land was coming to life, enriched with the spirit of her people.

Snow Flint examined the newly revealed shrine. "Do you see this image with the long tail?" he asked. "It is of a great spirit who had become lost wandering the sky. Do you remember the image we had near our old home?" "Yes", replied Wind Feather. "It was alone in the north canyon." "It was alone because these spirits often bring great misfortune." "Then why did the ancestors place this image here, so close to the moon?" queried Wind Feather. "Because the sky spirits are dangerous, and very powerful. The moon has charge over all her sky children. She is the only one who can calm the strength of a wandering sky spirit. And it is good for another reason . . ."

"Because the power of the Wanderer can be used by the moon; it can make her stronger," Wind Feather said with confidence.

"Yes. You have been paying attention. We can use this image in the moon ritual. There are just a few things we have to do first. Hand me my bag." Wind Feather helped Snow Flint ready the tools of the moon ritual. A number of women were due to give birth in the coming months and it

was necessary to appeal to the moon for maternal strength and healthy births. The Sky Mother would look after the spirits of the babies coming into the physical world. She would keep them healthy and instruct them in the process of birth. Knowing the power of the Wanderer would strengthen the moon in her tasks made Wind Feather happy. She loved blessing and purifying the new infants; it was a ritual she always looked forward to.

NATURAL FEATURES

USE OF NATURAL ROCK FEATURES IN PETROGLYPH DEPICTION

Very often the petroglyphs of east/central Arizona were created utilizing a natural feature of the rock face.

The most recognizable rock feature used by the petroglyph creators were naturally occurring gas bubbles in the basalt rock that appeared as small pockets. These pockets were often used as the eyes of figures in the case of anthropomorphs and zoomorphs.

Almost any feature that naturally occurred in the rock was used as a part of the depiction. A natural crack in the surface of the stone might have been used to represent the horizon, a trail, a river or level of emergence/existence. Often the natural feature of the rock would encourage the glyph maker to enhance the feature and create an image. A foliation in the stone that resembled part of the anatomy would often be enhanced by chiseling or pecking to create the completed image. Photo 65 is a good example. The basalt surface was foliated in the shape of the sole of the foot and the glyph maker added the toes completing the depiction.

Early petroglyph researchers tended to largely ignore natural rock features and focused only on the human created parts of the depiction. Natural features exhibited by the rock face are a very important contextual part of why the petroglyph was created. Prehistorically, the sought after power, the sympathetic magic associated with the glyph's creation, was greater if the rock face beckoned the image. This is similar to the Zuni use of the fetish. The Zuni create the small animal images as a charm for hunting both on the physical level and the spiritual. However, if they were fortunate enough to encounter a natural stone that resembled the animal, this stone had far more power than one that they had created.

The face of the stone itself was an important natural necessity for the creation of a petroglyph. The surface had to be smooth and have enough area to allow for the depiction and with sufficient patina to peck through to create it. Interestingly, areas with large rock surfaces and thick patina were not always utilized for the creation of petroglyphs even though the area was used for hunting and spiritual activities for centuries as is evident by other nearby cultural assemblages. Often one rock face will be crowded with glyphs and another seemingly better surface a few feet away will be blank. Many of the narrow canyons in the Upper Little Colorado area will exhibit petroglyphs almost exclusively on the north side of the rock faces. Just east of the Little Colorado River near Raven Site Ruins there is a wide canyon with abundant basalt surfaces which would have been ideal for petroglyph depictions and yet it seemed, none were created. Further survey revealed a small area in the canyon that was used as a shrine site, a place of spiritual experience where small offerings were left in stone niches. The shrine site area displayed many beautiful petroglyphs. It would seem that placing petroglyphs other than in proximity to the shrine was taboo.

The position of the rock face in relation to the sun, the four cardinal directions, and the prehistoric use of the area in general all seem to be relevant to the placement of glyphs.

Some natural or embellished features encountered in the surface of the stone served a more pragmatic function. Very often in the petroglyph areas one will discover cup stones, enhanced water tanks and rubbing stones.

Cup stones are small cup-shaped depressions carved or pecked into the surface of a large horizontal surface. They are frequently found amidst petroglyph areas. These may have served as mortars for grinding; either for food preparation in the field, sort of an on location metate, or pigments, as their small size would suggest. At well protected petroglyph sites it is not uncommon to find not only petroglyphs but often a few pictographs in sheltered alcoves. The pecked and chiseled petroglyphs may have been embellished with colored pigments prehistorically. In the unprotected areas open to weathering, these pigments would not have survived the ravages of time.

Enhanced water tanks are another semi-natural feature often encountered anywhere that prehistoric hunting or travel occurred in the arid Southwest. Any large horizontal stone surface where rainwater would naturally collect would often be modified by deepening the natural center depression or by adding grooves so that more water would accumulate. By knowing the location of these tanks it is possible to travel great distances from other more permanent water sources.

Rubbing stones are another feature which can be found utilizing a large horizontal rock surface. The nature of these features and how they were actually used prehistorically is still somewhat of a mystery. A large, gently concave, horizontal rock surface will exhibit evidence of rubbing over a wide area. Several of these features in the stone have been discovered south of Raven Site Ruins in east/central Arizona. They are found in association with abundant petroglyphs and cup stones. This area was undoubtedly utilized for several centuries by the prehistoric inhabitants of Raven Site Pueblo and their neighbors up and down the Little Colorado River. These large rubbing stones appear to have been repeatedly abraded from contact with a softer material such as leather. They may have been used to dress hides or butcher game. During the process of butchering a large game animal the smooth concave surface of the stone may have served as a table and the sloping sides to accommodate the collection of blood in the center depression. Defleshing a hide is another postulated use for these large rubbing stones.

Photo 61. Petroglyph from north of Raven Site Ruins in east / central Arizona showing an anthropomorph in the "prayer / blessing" stance created by utilizing two natural basalt gas bubbles which serve as eyes.

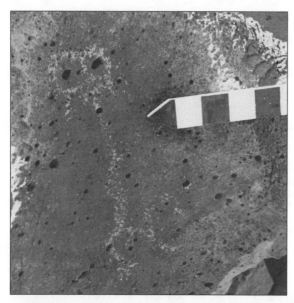

Photo 62. Petroglyph from north of Raven Site Ruins in east/central Arizona showing an anthropomorphic figure pecked around two basalt gas bubbles which create the eyes.

Photo 63. Petroglyph from north of Raven Site Ruins in east/central Arizona illustrating a mountain lion stalking his prey. The prey animal shown in profile was created utilizing a natural feature in the stone as the eye.

Photo 64. Petroglyph from north of Raven Site Ruins in east/central Arizona showing Kokopelli with insect features. The depiction utilizes a natural gas bubble in the stone for the eye.

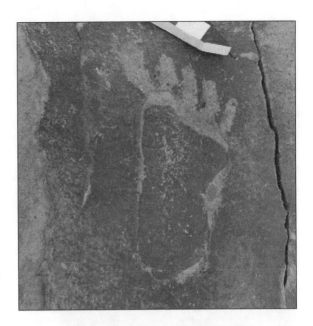

Photo 65. *Petroglyph from north of Raven Site Ruins in east / central Arizona. A large footprint was created using a natural exfoliation in the basalt. The petroglyph maker simply added the toes.*

Photo 66. *Petroglyph from north of Raven Site Ruins in east / central Arizona showing a three-fingered and toed anthropomorph in the "prayer / blessing" stance. The feet of the figure were pecked on the lower adjoining rock surface. The edge between the two rock faces may represent the division between one level of existence / emergence and the next. The figure is emerging up to the next level.*

Photo 67. *Petroglyph from east of Raven Site Ruins along the Upper Little Colorado River. Early historic use of the area is evident by this petroglyph. "Juan Montolla" pecked his name into the basalt in the year A.D. 1752. The dated panel and, only a few yards away, the ruins of his stone homestead still remain. Juan utilized a natural anomaly in the stone to create the "O".*

Photo 68. Cup stones from east of Raven Site Ruins in east/central Arizona. These small mortars may have been used to grind and/or moisten pigments to enhance petroglyphs or to prepare food in the field.

Photo 69. Enhanced water tank from east of Raven Site Ruins in east/central Arizona. Any large center-sloping rock surface could be modified to create a catch basin for life supporting water in the arid Southwest. Knowing the location of these miniature oases would enable the hunter or trader to travel far from more permanent water sources.

Photo 70. Rubbing Stone from north of Raven Site Ruins in east/central Arizona. These large rock surfaces appear to have been abraded by a softer pliable material such as leather. They may have been used for dressing skins or butchering game animals.

RITUAL USE OF NATURAL FEATURES

There are images or ideas having their origins in the minds of people, and there are images that have their origins in the natural world. The latter was traditionally regarded as more powerful than the former.

If an image was found to occur naturally on a stone, it was perceived as the product of the greater mind and spirit of nature. As a product of the natural spirit, it was connected, like offspring to the parent, to the spirit of nature. With a direct connection to the spirit, naturally occurring images were great sources of power that, if incorporated into petroglyphs, would make available to those petroglyph images a greater reservoir of power.

The natural image may have also been incorporated as a means of honoring the spirits of a particular stone or place. Honoring the "place" may have been a method of harmonizing with the spiritual elements having their origins in that place. If a shaman wanted to gain a greater connection with the spirits dwelling in a spring, the natural features near the spring would be made part of a ritual shrine. In this manner the shrine became spiritually connected to the spring, allowing the shaman to tap into the spring's power.

In some cases the incorporation of natural features may have been opportunistic. The carver of the petroglyph simply used some available features of the rock to save himself some work. Because of the perceptions of animism, the use of rock features would not have diminished the power of the petroglyph because the rock would have had its own spirit, just as powerful as the shaman-produced image.

SHRINE SITES, THE POWER OF THE PLACE

During our survey work gathering the hundreds of petroglyph photos presented in this volume we discovered several petroglyph sites that exhibited unique features. It was frequently observed that the petroglyphs were confined to one small area of a large canyon even though the rock throughout the canyon had sufficient patina upon which to easily create petroglyphs in several other areas. Very often when this was observed, all of the petroglyphs were pecked near unusual rock features such as caves, or arched niches near caves, or places in the canyon where large pockets in the rock face created naturally protected areas.

When viewing petroglyphs, the natural features of the rock face often are included in the depiction as part of the story that the panel illustrates. Gas pockets in the basalt become the eyes of anthropomorphs and zoomorphs and horizontal cracks and crevasses become the horizon. The people believed that any naturally occurring feature of the stone held more power, more magic than one that was created by man.

This is the nature of shrine sites. Special places, naturally occurring caves, isolated and unique eclectic boulders and stone pockets made by the gods invited spiritual use by the prehistoric people.

One unique rock feature that is very common to shrine sites is the presence of a pocket in the wall of the canyon that is arched at the top and flat at the bottom. These natural niches in the stone were used as places of offering. The prehistoric people would leave gifts of turquoise beads, shell and other valuables to accompany their prayers.

Shrine sites offered the power of the place to the prehistoric people of the Southwest. To the petroglyph researcher, they offer not only a myriad of images pecked into the stone surrounding the shrine sites, but also a glimpse of the colors that were used to accompany the petroglyphs. At shrine sites that are protected from the elements of weathering, pictographs, or painted imagery, often survive the ravages of time. Pictographs are a rare find in the field and discovering a small cave bright with blue turquoise and red ocher paintings is a thrilling experience.

It has long been my suspicion that many of the petroglyphs throughout the Southwest were not only pecked into the stone surface as we see them today, but that they were also prehistorically painted and enhanced with colors. Canyons where petroglyphs are found almost always have cup stones present. These small cup-shaped depressions can be found on large horizontal rocks. It has been speculated that they were used to grind food in the field, but they may actually have been used to grind pigments to enhance the petroglyphs. The pigments could not survive the elements of wind, rain and sun in open areas.

During our survey we discovered a shrine site south of Holbrook, Arizona. This natural square indentation in the canyon face revealed several wonderful petroglyphs. One of the petroglyphs within the shrine itself still exhibits the turquoise pigment that brightened it many centuries ago.

Photo 71. Shrine site south of Holbrook, Arizona showing several of the naturally occurring features that are often common to shrine sites. The large square natural pocket in the wall of the canyon serves as the shrine. The area above and within the pocket is covered with petroglyphs and some still exhibit pigment enhancement. To the right of the large pocket in the photograph there is an arched niche in the rock wall. These niches served as places to leave offerings of shell and stone.

Photo 72. Floor of the shrine site shown in Photo 71.

Photo 73. Shrine site south of Holbrook, Arizona. This large, square feature in the side of the canyon served as a prehistoric shrine. The images are all pictographs. The pigments are red ocher / iron oxide, white kaoline, and black and grey charcoal. There are crane images, hunt magic, a serpent, an anthropomorph in transition and several unusual geometric forms. At the top left of the geometric cluster there are several very unusual Kokopellis or flute players. This shrine site is well protected and fortunately the pigments have survived the ravages of time. The shrine is now home to several mud swallows. Their nests can be seen at the top left of the photo.

Photo 74. Shrine site south of Raven Site Ruins in east / central Arizona. Often a large eclectic boulder would serve as a powerful gathering place for the prehistoric people. This boulder creates a roof over a small cave beneath. The surface of the stone is covered with imagery including a very large serpent (upper left), bird tracks and anthropomorphs in prayer. In front of this boulder the shrine was enhanced prehistorically by the addition of a small stone room. The remains of the walls and the doorway are still visible. The arrow in the photograph is in the doorway.

Photo 75. Shrine site north of St. Johns, Arizona. At the head of a canyon there are several large water-eroded pockets and caves. These are covered with petroglyphs. Each pocket served as a powerful place to communicate with the gods.

Photo 76. Hand and footholds were carved into the sandstone to make access easier into the shrine site shown in Photo 75.

Photo 77. Natural niches in the stone are found nearby the shrine shown in photo 75. These small naturally occurring openings in the canyon walls served as places to leave offerings to the gods.

Photo 78. Shrine site east of Raven Site Ruins in east/central Arizona. This shrine has the power of a natural cave in the basalt. Associated petroglyphs include a net or fence, emergence depictions and several geometric forms.

Photo 79. Arched niches in the canyon wall very near the shrine shown in Photo 78. These niches are where the gods received small offerings from the prehistoric people.

Photo 80. Bits of ceramic, shell and stone from offerings made in the niches shown in Photo 79 and associated with the shrine in Photo 78 can still be found.

Photo 81. Rock alignments south of Raven Site Ruins in east/central Arizona. Two of these stone arrangements are located within 50 meters of each other; one is oriented due north and the other is oriented east and west. These features are believed to have been used prehistorically during ceremonial rites of passage.

RITUAL ASPECTS OF SHRINES

There were some rituals that the shaman was capable of enacting regardless of location. These rituals used energies that the shaman had at his disposal or was capable of calling upon alone. Shrines, however, were different in that they were tools of shamanic magic that were location dependent. The shaman could not bring the shrine to a place of ritual. The shaman had to travel to the shrine in order to use its particular power in ritual. Because animists believed all things were vested with spirit, they could judge the relative quality of spirit contained in a particular thing or place. Shrines were established because a shaman or some other spiritual practitioner had judged a location or object to be the locus of powerful or useful spiritual energy.

Shrines were powerful because they were locations of spiritual power. From these locations the shaman could use the natural energies that had their origins in sources that were greater than the shaman alone. Shrines were not tools; they were more like co-generators of spiritual power.

Shrine rituals sought to work through the shrine to accomplish specific tasks with the shrine's natural energy. This shrine energy could be used alone or could be used to complement the energy of the shaman.

The petroglyphs found at shrines were used to introduce specific shamanic concepts that could be used to shape the power of the shrine. If a net, rattle, or moon image was placed on a shrine, the power of the shrine could be channeled through the image to empower the normal effects of the image's ritual concept. In the same way, hunt magic would gain the power of the shrine in addition to that of the shaman if its petroglyph components were made part of a shrine.

It is easy to see why some shrine locations inspired the spirit of the tribal shaman. They were simply physically impressive. However, the reason for the origin of some sites is harder to determine. Smooth rock faces that were simply good locations for petroglyph production may have evolved into shrines through a process of cumulative use of the same location. After a period of time, the sheer number and density of images would have qualified the site as a shrine.

CELESTIAL IMAGERY:
SUNS, STARS, COMETS, THE ECLIPSE, AND SUPERNOVA

Petroglyphs in the Southwest often represent stars. An outlined cross or outlined double cross is believed to represent Quetzalcoatl. This Mesoamerican god ascended into the heavens and became Venus, or the morning star. The outlined double cross is believed to also represent this idea, adding the element of both the morning and evening star to the imagery.

Petroglyphs that represent the sun are often confused with glyphs that may have other meaning. Petroglyphs with a circle center and radiating lines are usually interpreted as images of the sun. However, many of these glyphs may represent flowers, or other concepts. The sun in pueblo thought is identified as a male figure, i.e., a father symbol and is often identified by the eagle. The moon is identified as a female symbol and is often represented by the rabbit. Most cultures including the prehistoric Southwestern Indians, Mesoamericans, and Chinese "see" a rabbit in the moon as opposed to the Western idea of a "man" in the moon. The earth is also symbolized by the female, i.e., Mother Earth.

Spectacular events in the sky have been recorded in the rock art of the Southwest.

Comets are not commonly depicted in the rock imagery probably due to their rare appearances in the sky. Some Southwestern cultures interpret the comet as the White Coyote crossing the sky and his sighting results in death and destruction (Zigmond 1977).

Petroglyphs illustrating solar and lunar eclipses have been discovered, but the best graphic examples of these events can be found on Mimbres ceramics dating from A.D. 950 to A.D. 1150. The symbol of the eagle or bird of prey represents the sun and the symbol of the rabbit represents the moon. Several Mimbres bowls illustrate the rabbit being eaten by the eagle. These depictions are believed to represent the lunar eclipse.

Petroglyphs depicting the Supernova which occurred in the Taurus system on July 5, A.D.

1054 have been found in several locations throughout the Southwest including Northern Arizona and Abo Monument & Chaco Canyon in New Mexico. Other depictions of this spectacular event are found on the ceramics of the Mimbres Indians.

Photo 82 (left) and 83 (below-right). The outlined cross is believed to represent the Mesoamerican god Quetzalcoatl who ascended into the sky and became Venus, the morning star. The outlined double cross incorporates the idea of both the morning and evening stars.

Photo 84 (left) and 85 (below left). Petroglyphs that are believed to represent the sun often resemble other symbols. A central circle with radiating lines could indeed represent the sun. However, these images could also be stars or flowers.

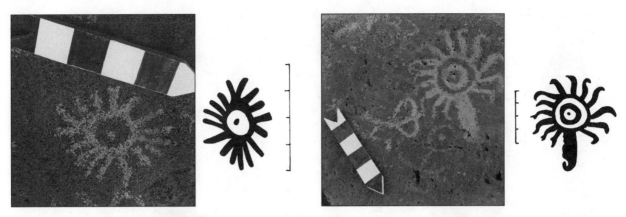

Photos 86 and 87. Petroglyphs from the Upper Little Colorado region that resemble images of the sun but may actually represent flowers, specifically the tobacco blossom. Tobacco was a frequent offering to the gods and smoking ceremonies played a large role in prehistoric life ways.

Figures 152 and 153. Tobacco flower symbol painted on San Bernardo jars dating A.D. 1625 to A.D. 1680 interpreted by the Hopi as the symbol representing a division of the Eagle phratry (Stephen 1890 [Patterson 1994]).

Photo 88 (left) and Figure 154 (right). Photo on the left is a petroglyph from north of Raven Site Ruins showing a symbol that resembles a sun symbol but that has been interpreted by the Hopi to represent the game "Tugh-ti-wiki" in which the young boys and girls, hooking fingers, attempt to drag each other across an imaginary line. Figure 154 illustrates the same symbol painted on a San Bernardo jar (Stephen 1890 [Patterson 1994]).

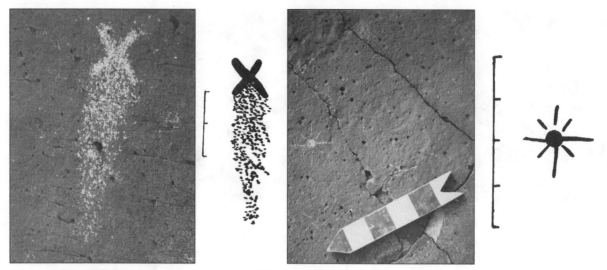

Photos 89 and 90. Petroglyphs from west of Eagar, Arizona showing very graphic comet and a small star.

Figures 155 and 156. Mimbres bowls dating from A.D. 950 to A.D. 1150 showing a rabbit being eaten by a bird of prey. These images are believed to represent the lunar eclipse, the rabbit representing the moon and the eagle the sun (Robbins/Westmoreland unpublished manuscript, LeBlanc 1983).

Northern
Arizona

Abo Monument
New Mexico

Chaco Canyon
New Mexico

Figure 157. Supernova petroglyphs of the Southwest which may represent the star explosion in the Taurus system on July 5th, A.D. 1054 (Patterson 1992).

Figure 158. Mimbres bowl dating between A.D. 1000 and A.D. 1070 showing the lunar rabbit in the sky with another object. This second body in the sky which exhibits 23 rays is believed to represent the supernova of A.D. 1054. This guest star in the Taurus system would have been visible for 23 consecutive days (Robbins/Westmoreland unpublished manuscript, LeBlanc 1983).

RITUAL ASPECTS OF CELESTIAL IMAGERY

Celestial images were the petroglyph representations of beings or deities who inhabited the spiritual world of the sky. The mythic portrayal of these beings defined their nature and consequent uses in ritual. Petroglyph illustrations of these beings served to channel their particular energies for shamanic use.

The sun, in addition to its masculine spiritual qualities, was also thought to be a doorway to the spirit world. This was a celestial version of the terrestrial sipapu. The sipapu was a deep round hole found in kivas. This hole was symbolic of the hole from which the tribes emerged at the beginning of this world. A symbolic representation of the sipapu could tap into the energy of creation present at the time of emergence. The sun sipapu could be used to tap into the spiritual creation energy of the sky spirit world.

The moon was a pool of feminine energy. The moon could strengthen any feminine endeavor, be it childbirth or the rituals of womanhood. The moon symbols could also be used by the shaman to lend nurturing strength to crops and other living things.

In addition to the permanent celestial figures, the petroglyph panels also recorded those passing figures of the sky. There are images of comets, falling stars, novas, and possibly the aurora borealis. These images were recorded in stone because they represented spectacular natural events ripe with the power of the spirit world. What specific spiritual power the recording shaman attributed to the fleeting figures is uncertain, though we can assume they were used as a special component of ritual.

Shaman's Mark

"Just as the bear or the cougar leave their marks, you must leave yours. If you are to work with the spirit of this land you must be connected to it," said Snow Flint as he placed prayer feathers on the rocks above a petroglyph footprint.

Wind Feather examined the large yellow-painted image, the newest of several footprints on the stone. The print had six toes representing the shaman's sixth sense of spirit.

Snow Flint drew a circle on the dry ground in front of the foot-stone. "You must stay within this line. This will be your space. You will be safe in here and the spirits will feel free to approach you. You must not eat and you must contemplate the spirit of this sacred ground. If you do this, the spirits will come to know you. Then you may seek their help," said Snow Flint.

"Will they make themselves known to me?" Wind Feather asked apprehensively.

"They may. On the second or third day you may hear sounds and see movement in the corner of your eyes. This will be the spirits coming to see you. If your heart is pure, they may come to you in a vision or dream and present themselves to you."

"I will wait for them."

Wind Feather sat down in her space. She let her body relax into the ground and become a part of the shrine-filled plateau.

Snow Flint picked up his bag and said "You must open yourself. I will be back for you in three days."

"You will find me here," answered Wind Feather .

After only a few minutes Wind Feather thought she could almost hear voices in the wind and feel the powerful spirits of the stones. She pushed down the excitement that swelled within her. She knew that she had to maintain a calm and focused mind if she was to invite the spirits to reveal themselves.

With renewed determination she relaxed. The greatest challenge would be controlling herself, maintaining the proper frame of mind, and not making the spirits flee her disruptive enthusiasm. Behind her she could feel the yellow shaman's footprint, her print, calling to the spirits in her name.

TRACKS

FOOTPRINTS

There is an abundance of human footprints encountered at most petroglyph sites. In the Upper Little Colorado Drainage there are hundreds of depictions of human feet.

Bare human footprints combined with a spiral or wavy line often represent a trail or mark a path; see ("Trail Markers".) Footprints are often seen in a series which could represent a trail or path taken. Very often single or pairs of footprints are included in large petroglyph panels combined with a myriad of other symbols. These may represent a journey either physical or spiritual. Examples of single footprints included in complex panels have been found where the footprint is greatly elongated. Modern Hopi informants conclude that these represent particular clans (clan identity was determined by other glyphs on the same panel) and those clans came to mark the spot after a very long journey illustrated by the elongation of the footprint glyph.

The majority of these depictions show the normal foot with five toes. However, there are several examples of human footprints with six toes. This could represent an actual deformity that was either feared or revered. Physical deformities that were genetically transmitted such as six toes and dwarfism were revered in prehistoric societies and individuals exhibiting these characteristics held unique social positions such as shaman or spiritual leader.

One rock art panel discovered near Raven Site Ruins shows several human footprints. One of these prints has the added appendages of arms and a head extending from the big and little toes and the third toe. The arms are raised in a "prayer" stance. This personification could indicate a greater significance to the human footprint glyph than was previously assigned.

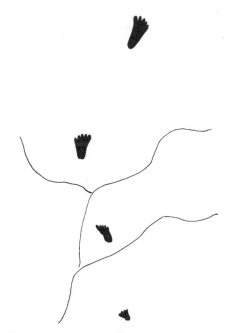

Figure 159. Petroglyphs of a series of footprints across different basalt rocks (Schaafsma 1980).

Photo 91. Petroglyph panel north of St. Johns, Arizona showing a large footprint with other symbols. The wavy lines included with these footprints may indicate a journey either physical or spiritual.

Photo 92. *Petroglyph from north of St. Johns, Arizona. Two very large footprints are included within the context of a large panel.*

Photo 93. *Petroglyph from south of Holbrook, Arizona showing a pair of footprints within a complex panel.*

Photo 94. *Petroglyph panel from south of Holbrook, Arizona. This elongated footprint has been translated by Hopi informants as representing a very, very long journey taken by a clan. This translation is further reinforced by the long wavy line connected to the spiral accompanying the footprint.*

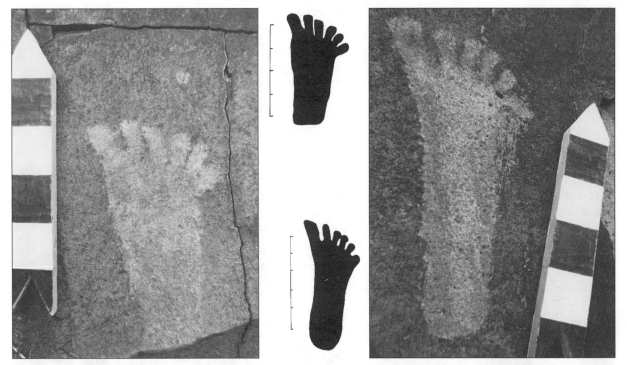

Photo 95 and 96. *Footprints with six toes from north of Raven Site Ruins, Arizona. This genetically transmitted deformity was feared and revered in prehistoric societies.*

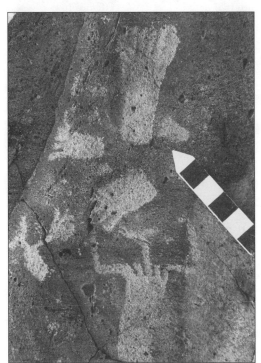

Photo 97. *Petroglyph from north of Raven Site Ruins, Arizona. The footprint at the bottom has been enhanced with upraised arms indicating "prayer" or "blessing" and a head extending from the third toe.*

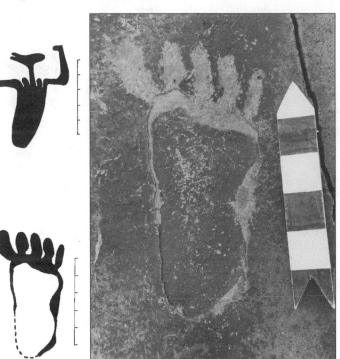

Photo 98. *Petroglyph from north of Raven Site Ruins, Arizona. This very large footprint was created by adding only the toes to a natural exfoliation in the basalt.*

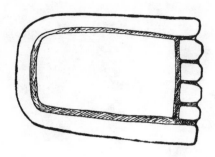

Figure 160. Stone palette in the shape of a footprint or bear's paw from excavations at the Galaz site in the Mimbres Valley. Notice that this palette exhibits six toes. The bear is associated with healing powers (LeBlanc 1983).

Figure 161. Mimbres bowl showing an encounter between a hunter and a bear. The footprints which encircle the depiction probably represent the hunter's journey either on a physical or spiritual level (LeBlanc 1983).

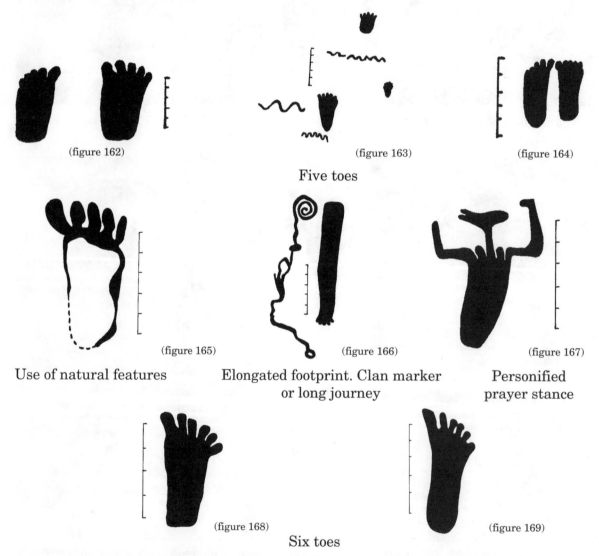

(figure 162)

(figure 163)

(figure 164)

Five toes

(figure 165)

(figure 166)

(figure 167)

Use of natural features

Elongated footprint. Clan marker or long journey

Personified prayer stance

(figure 168)

(figure 169)

Six toes

Figure 161. Footprints from the Upper Little Colorado area in East/Central Arizona. Footprints are frequently included in large petroglyph panels, combined with many other symbols.

RITUAL ASPECTS OF FOOTPRINTS

Footprints, like handprints, could have been signature marks that drew blessing from a shrine or a sacred place. The footprint firmly established the connection of an individual, or symbolically a group of people, to a source of spiritual energy. A shaman would conduct a ceremony activating the connection of an individual to a footprint for purposes of personal power. The power gained from sacred sites was general in nature. Therefore, it was probably used by individuals who needed a boost in their native capabilities. Tribal leaders, traders, or those who faced challenging circumstances might have petitioned the shaman for personal empowerment.

Footprints could also be associated with trails or traveling. They could mark or symbolically refer to a trail, a long trek, or migration. The last is true of Hopi interpretations of footprints. Images of mythic migrations may have been a source of the transformative power of creation. This power could have been used by the shaman to protect travelers or to bring success to tribal traders and travelers.

The spirit journey of the shaman may have been represented by footprints. This possibility is bolstered by the frequency of six-toed prints associated with shamanic or spiritual personages. Many tribes used uncommon physical attributes to recognize those called to the practice of shamanism. These signs were dwarfism, epilepsy, and extra digits to name a few.

The footprint petroglyph may have been a tool to help the shaman to make a journey into the spirit world. A shaman entering a trance at a shrine site with footprints may have used the sympathetic power of the footprints to guide the spirit journey to a specific supernatural destination. Once the shaman had accomplished his or her task, the footprint may have acted as an anchor to the physical world of the shrine site.

ANIMAL TRACKS

Petroglyphs of animal tracks are quite common. Most of the track representations are easily identified as to the species of the animal. In many cases it is easier to identify what animal is being depicted in a petroglyph by a track representation than it is when the prehistoric people pecked the image of the whole animal.

The skill of tracking animals is vital to a successful hunt, especially when large game is the quarry. It is clearly evident that the creators of the petroglyphs graphically knew how to identify one animal from another by their tracks. Many of the petroglyph panels create the image of a successful hunt, either to insure success of a future hunt, or to record one that has succeeded.

Track representations are not always linear. Often just a single track or pair of tracks will be pecked into the stone surface. The image of the track of a bear or mountain lion may have been sufficient to represent the idea or power of that animal.

Often track representations are identified by modern Hopi informants as representing clan symbols or identities.

Photos 99 and 100. Petroglyphs from north of Raven Site Ruins in East/Central Arizona showing a pair of bear tracks and a single mountain lion track.

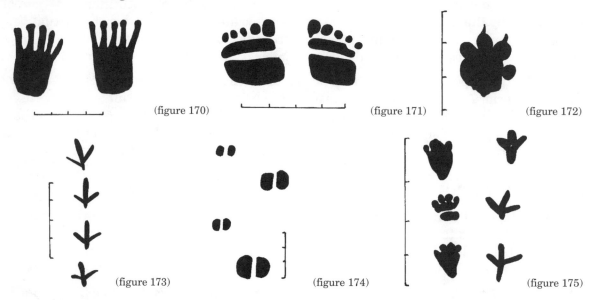

(figure 170) (figure 171) (figure 172)

(figure 173) (figure 174) (figure 175)

Figures 170-175. Animal tracks from the Upper Little Colorado River area.

RITUAL ASPECTS OF ANIMAL TRACKS

For ritual use, tracks were as good as representations of the whole animal. The image had only to have a clear connection to an animal in order for it to be a channel to the spiritual power of the animal. Tribal shaman would also use small parts of a particular animal, such as claws, fur or teeth, in rituals that depend upon the power of that animal. Tracks served the same purpose as claws or teeth in ritual.

Tracks may also have been clan or society symbols. These marks recorded the journey of a clan member to a shrine or pilgrimage spot. Clan symbols were also used in rituals to strengthen a clan or to use the traditional spiritual power of a clan. When clans and societies of the pueblos began taking charge for particular ceremonies, clans gained the associated spiritual power. Consequently, clan symbols became vested with the powers of the clan and were useful tools in shamanic rituals that required the use those powers.

Rebirth

Wind Feather sat on the woven yucca mat near the hearth of Snow Flint's pueblo room. The smooth plastered walls were covered with the images of the various clans, the four directions and the spirit helpers of Snow Flint. Ceramic canteens, gourds, and leather bags hung from pegs, casting long shadows that moved with the fire's rhythm over the images. The packed-dirt floor was covered with a variety of frayed mats, pottery containers, and the tools of the shaman's trade.

The old shaman sat on his sleeping mat with a heavy pelt wrapped around his shoulders. Snow Flint had placed a flat sandstone working slab before him and was grinding a piece of limonite into small mounds of bright yellow powder. Wind Feather noticed that there was little food in the room and that her teacher was looking gaunt.

The first winter in a new land is always hard, so Snow Flint had told Wind Feather. The tribe had not yet discovered the best places to forage or hunt. The crops had only been marginal because some of the soil was bad and the irrigation system was unfinished. The people were living on small meals of dried maize and beans, supplemented with what the hunters were able to provide.

Next winter would be better. The people would know the land better and would be able store more food. But for now it was vital that the hunters continue to be successful. The game had to be replenished so that the people would survive the season.

"Don't worry. You know the chants. You will perform the rituals very well," said Snow Flint without looking up from his grinding.

"I know the words, but I'm not sure I'll be successful for all the game. It's so important now." Wind Feather said, her voice filled with self-doubt.

"You are not just speaking to the game. You are speaking to the Great Spirit and asking that it do its own will. Rebirth is the will of the Great Spirit. It only needs you to fulfill our part of the task."

"I still wish you were coming with me."

"It's time that you do some of the rituals on your own. You are ready," he reassured her.

Wind Feather reached for the hawk fetish that hung from her neck. When she touched it, she could see the hawk-spirit that came to her during the summer. She could feel the sunlight and the light stroking of wings on her face. For a moment she could see herself sitting in her circle of space,

next to her shamanic print. Her spirit had glided over the shrines, over the plateau and the pueblo. When she found herself back in the circle, she had seen the light image of a hawk on the shrine. She had cleaned that shrine and had performed ritual there, but never had she noticed that image before.

Shaking herself, Wind Feather came back to the reality of her duty to her tribe.

"Go now. The sun is beginning to show himself." Snow Flint said to her with his knotted hand on her shoulder.

"Yes. I'm ready."

With food, water and her tools, Wind Feather climbed the now familiar path to the plateau of shrines. She had two long days of solitary ritual ahead of her. The game rebirthing rituals were among the most important of the year. The hunters needed these rituals to prevent vengeful spirits from tormenting them. Through the game rebirth rituals, the tribe entered into an agreement with the game. An understanding that in exchange for their flesh, the tribe would perform the rituals necessary for the game's rebirth, a chance to live again and to feed the tribe again. Wind Feather would execute a set of rituals for each of the species of game. The petroglyphs of the hunt shrine would allow her to reach out to the spiritual energy of hunted animals through the process of ritual. These rituals would strengthen and maintain the cycle of rebirth that directed game to the spirit world where the Great Spirit could give the animals new lives, fulfilling the tribe's obligation.

Gliding above in slow circles, Wind Feather saw a hunting hawk. "You'll help me. You understand the importance of hunting," she said to the confident figure above her.

With steady, sure steps Wind Feather climbed closer to the shrines.

ANIMALS

QUADRUPEDS

The four-legged animals that are represented in the rock imagery of the Upper Little Colorado region do not exhibit the variety that was expected at the beginning of this study. A prehistoric society that relied upon hunting for much of its sustenance would assumably create images of the game animals to draw the mana of the animal and assure success in the hunt. Other rock art animal images would represent clans that associated themselves with specific animals. Both of the above scenarios were encountered in the petroglyph depictions from the region, but only a fraction of the total four-legged animal index was represented. Nearly all of the quadrupeds represented were large game such as elk, deer, antelope, bighorn sheep, bear, and mountain lion. None of the smaller game animals that made up the bulk of the prehistoric diet were found on the rock art. This is probably because the smaller game is not that difficult to successfully hunt. Setting out to hunt rabbits was probably no more demanding than heading down to the corn field to irrigate. On the other hand, hiking several days into the mountains in quest of elk, stalking the animal, shooting, tracking the wounded game, then skinning, quartering, and manuporting several hundred pounds of meat back to the pueblo, is far more laborious and would require the help of the gods in the form of mana, or sacred spiritual energy.

Deer and Elk

Depictions illustrating deer, elk and antelope shown with the hunter shooting arrows at his quarry are not uncommon (see "Bow and Arrow"). These rock art panels may be documenting a successful hunt, or they may represent the hoped for results of a hunt about to commence.

Photos 101 (left) and 102 (right). Petroglyphs from south of Holbrook, Arizona showing antlered quadrupeds. Photo 101 probably represents a running deer. Photo 102 includes elk or deer and a small spirit or spirit helper in the upper left area of the glyph.

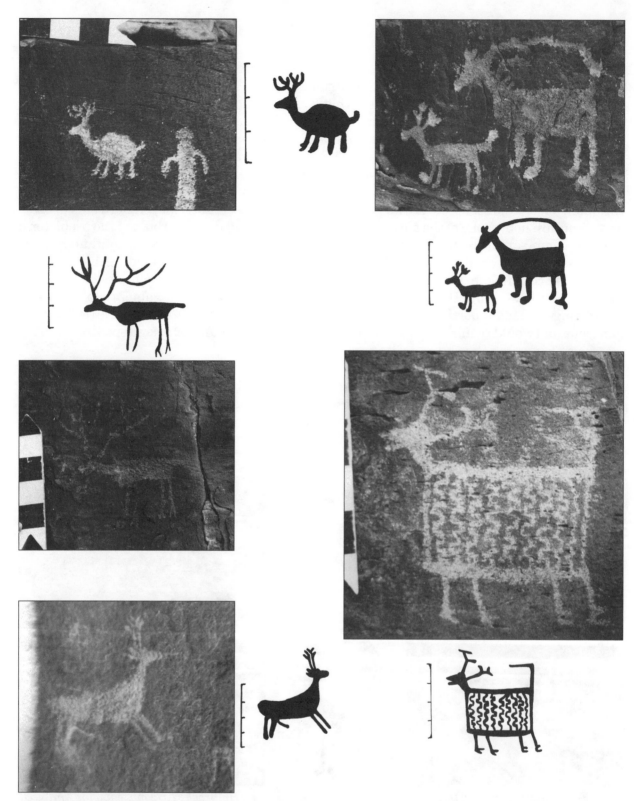

Photos 103-107. Petroglyphs from the Upper Little Colorado River area showing antlered quadrupeds. These depictions probably represent deer and elk, as opposed to quadrupeds with antlers that are not as branched, such as antelope or bighorn sheep.

Antelope, Bighorn Sheep, Mountain Goats

Many petroglyph researchers are quick to classify many of the common quadrupeds seen on the rock imagery of the Southwest as mountain goats or bighorn sheep. Indeed there seems to be an overabundance of goats and sheep according to these interpretations. However, very few mountain goat or bighorn sheep bones have been found amongst the faunal assemblages from the trash middens of the pueblo ruins. These animals were not a common part of the diet. In fact, these animals held a supernatural significance according to pueblo mythology (Schaafsma 1981).

The mountain goat and bighorn sheep are represented in the rock imagery, probably due to this supernatural significance, but many of the images thought to be mountain sheep are probably representations of the antelope. Antelope images can be identified by their thin minimal horns and square-shaped bodies. The hooves are often represented as a paired appendage. The square body is often filled with geometric designs. Butchered antelope bones are a frequent discovery in the trash middens from the prehistoric ruin and they were a common part of the diet.

Photos 108 (left) and 109 (right). Petroglyphs showing bighorn sheep. These elusive animals held a supernatural significance in pueblo thought. They are not depicted on the rock imagery of the Southwest as frequently as some researchers have interpreted.

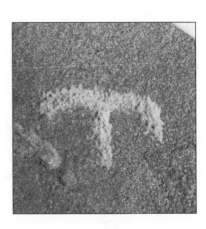

Photo 110. Petroglyph from north of St. Johns, Arizona showing the clan symbol that represents the bighorn sheep which depicts the curvature of the horns.

Photos 111 and 112. Petroglyphs from north of Raven Site Ruins in east/central Arizona showing quadrupeds that probably represent antelope. The square body is often filled with geometric designs.

With many of the quadrupeds found on the rock imagery of the Southwest it is very difficult to determine what species of animal that they represent. Most of the large game animals that are illustrated have distinctive attributes that give the researcher clues as to what specific animal is being depicted. Some, however, are a bit of a mystery. Photographs 113, 114, and 115 are petroglyphs from north of St. Johns, Arizona. All three depict an animal with nearly identical attributes, but the species is still indefinite. In all three examples the feet are facing forward as if the animal is running. The ears or horns and tails are all very similar as is the long snout. Photo 113 illustrates two animals. The smaller animal to the top left is virtually identical to the other examples. The larger more graphic animal at the bottom right of the photo may be a representation of the same quadruped. If indeed it is, then the species of all of these petroglyphs is probably antelope.

Photos 113 (top left), 114 (bottom left), and 115 (bottom right). Petroglyphs from north of St. Johns, Arizona showing quadrupeds with very similar attributes, but the species is still a mystery. Photo 113, with the larger more graphic depiction at the lower right may indicate that all of these hoofed animals are indeed antelope. Notice how the feet are all turned forward in an almost playful manner.

Bear

One excellent petroglyph of a bear has been discovered south of Holbrook, Arizona. This example exaggerates the feet of the bear and included on the panel is a very elongated bear track. Modern Hopi informants speculated that the bear clan traveled a long journey to arrive at the spot. Bear are associated with healing in pueblo mythology and the bear track is identified as a clan symbol.

Photos 116 (top) and 117 (bottom). Petroglyph from south of Holbrook, Arizona. Bear and elongated bear track. Bear are associated with healing and the bear track is identified as a clan symbol. The elongated bear track in Photo 116 has been interpreted by modern Hopi informants to mean that the bear clan traveled a very, very long way to arrive at the site.

Mountain Lions

There are numerous mountain lion depictions in the Upper Little Colorado River region, far more than any other quadruped. Distinguishing characteristics of these glyphs are an elongated body, long tail which is usually arched over the back of the animal, and either ball feet or feet that depict claws. In Hopi and Zuni mythology the mountain lion is symbolic of the north. In Mohave myth there are two lion figures who assist the Creator God; one of these lions has his tail up in the air and the other down (Johnson 1986).

Photo 118. Petroglyph from Lyman Lake State Park, Arizona. The mountain lion in this photo shows the tail over the back and clawed feet.

Photo 119. Petroglyph from north of Raven Site Ruins, Arizona shows a mountain lion tracking his prey. The tail is over the back and the figure has ball feet. His path is indicated by the trailing series of dots.

Photo 120. Petroglyph from north of St. Johns, Arizona shows two possible mountain lions. One with the tail over the back and the other with the tail down.

(figure 176)

(figure 177)

(figure 178)

(figure 179)

(figure 180)

(figure 181)

(figure 182)

(figure 183)

(figure 84)

(figure 185)

(figure 186)

(figure 187)

(figure 188)

Figures 176-188. Mountain lion petroglyphs from the Upper Little Colorado River area. Common elements are long tails arched over the back, elongated bodies and clawed or ball feet.

(figure 189)

(figure 190)

(figure 191)

(figure 192)

(figure 193)

(figure 194)

(figure 195)

(figure 196)

(figure 197)

(figure 198)

(figure 199)

(figure 200)

(figure 201)

(figure 202)

(figure 203)

(figure 204)

(figure 205)

Figures 189-205. Quadruped petroglyphs from the Upper Little Colorado River area. Many of these depictions are difficult to definitively identify according to species.

Figure 206. Mimbres bowl dating between A.D. 950 and A.D. 1150 showing a mountain lion with the classic tail over the back and clawed feet. The balled feet in many of the petroglyph depictions is probably a simplification of the clawed feet or pads of the feet of the lion (Brody 1977).

RITUAL ASPECTS OF QUADRUPEDS

The vast majority of large herd animals seen on petroglyph panels were used in the various types of hunt magic. The shaman controlled the spiritual power of the prey to make it more vulnerable to the skills of the hunter.

Seldom are the smaller hunted animals such as rabbits, squirrels or beaver seen in petroglyph panels. Small game were easy enough to hunt without the ritual help of the shaman. Such figures as the rabbit were usually produced for the type of specific power it represented, rather than to acquire the animal itself. The rabbit was often associated with the moon and hence with feminine power, whereas the beaver was often associated with rivers and water spirits.

The larger prey animals also had spiritual power and qualities that could be used by the shaman in rituals. Among several pueblo people, the elk is regarded as one of the bravest animals, therefore very useful in rituals that sought to instill bravery in warriors or others that might need it.

There were a number of animals seldom hunted for food yet often carved into the stone panels of the Southwest. Depictions of these animals were almost exclusively used by the shaman to ritually manipulate the powers of their particular natures. The cougar was a powerful source of hunt power, of strength and agility. The cougar image would be used in hunt magic only to empower the hunter against lesser prey. The bear was a source of strength and healing power. The bear image would be used to empower the shaman or to direct healing toward the sick.

The quadruped class of petroglyphs covered most of the primary animals that were used in the hunt and rebirth rituals of shamanism. These animals were the core of beings who existed in the symbiotic relationship of hunter-prey and human-animal. This symbiosis was based upon the shamanic rituals that would ensure those animals killed in the hunt would be reborn to live and to be hunted again. The animals supplied their bodies to the tribe and the shaman supplied the rituals that gave the animals new bodies and lives.

BIRDS

The petroglyphs of the Upper Little Colorado region abound with depictions of birds. Many of these can be identified according to species, specifically turkeys, cranes, quail, and parrots. Certain species characteristics, plumage and behaviors are associated with larger concepts in pueblo mythology as indicated by the context of the bird representations. Bird imagery is not confined to petroglyphs but is also abundantly seen painted on the ceramics and murals of the prehistoric Southwest.

In general, birds and feathers represent flight, that is, the ability to escape the bounds of the earth and transcend into the realm of the gods. They are often seen as messengers. Their feathers are included on the prayer sticks offered to the gods to enable the prayer to ascend to the sky.

Specifically, each species of bird may represent a more unique idea in prehistoric pueblo thought based upon the bird's inherent behaviors. Plumage form and color are also very important considerations. Colors have directional affiliations within the mythology of the Zuni, Hopi and other cultural groups occupying the Southwest.

Parrots

Parrots were traded to the inhabitants of the prehistoric Southwestern United States from as far south as central Mexico. These exotic birds were valued for their colorful plumage which was used in creating prayer sticks, ceremonial costuming and other paraphernalia. Large cages for raising parrots for extended trade have been excavated at Casas Grandes just south of the Mexican/American border. Elaborate parrot burials have been discovered in the prehistoric ruins of the greater Southwest. Parrots were valuable. They were exotic, colorful, verbal, and their behaviors and plumage were seen as powerful links to the world of the gods.

Photos 121 (left) and 122 (right). Petroglyphs from south of Holbrook, Arizona showing stylized parrots. These depictions are very similar to those found on the prehistoric ceramics of the Southwest. Parrots and other birds are often depicted with a horizontal surface or perch.

Parrots are sometimes associated with Kokopelli figures in rock art depictions, conjectured to be affiliated with Kokopelli's role as a trader of exotic goods.

Petroglyphs and ceramics depicting parrots are not uncommon. These depictions are usually stylized, exaggerating the sharply curved beak and long tail feathers. The body of the bird is often reduced to a simple triangle.

Photo 123 (left) shows a Kwakina Polychrome bowl dating from A.D. 1325 to A.D. 1400.

Photo 124 (left) shows a Pinnawa Glaze-on-white bowl dating between A.D. 1350 and A.D. 1450 (Cunkle 1994).

Photo 125 (left) is a petroglyph from south of Holbrook, Arizona illustrating an anthropomorph with a parrot in a hoop. Note the bullet hole that nearly obliterated the petroglyph. Unfortunately, vandalism like this is common.

Figures 207 (left) and 208 (right). Mimbres vessels dating between A.D. 950 and A.D. 1150 showing tamed parrots within hoops and parrot trainers. The female figure illustrated on both vessels is nearly identically depicted. All of the elements of the costume, the parrot mask with double lines on the cheek, the banded sash, the sandals and the staff are the same (Brody 1977 and 1983).

Cranes

Depictions of cranes are frequently seen in the rock imagery of the Southwest. Cranes can be easily identified by their long legs and long neck. The nature of the crane in the prehistoric mythology of the Southwest is not clearly understood. They are an underworld figure in both Mesoamerican and historic pueblo ideology and they are associated with water and the dead. They are often illustrated with other riparian elements such as fish which could simply be naturalistic. However, several ceramic depictions clearly indicate an affiliation with de-

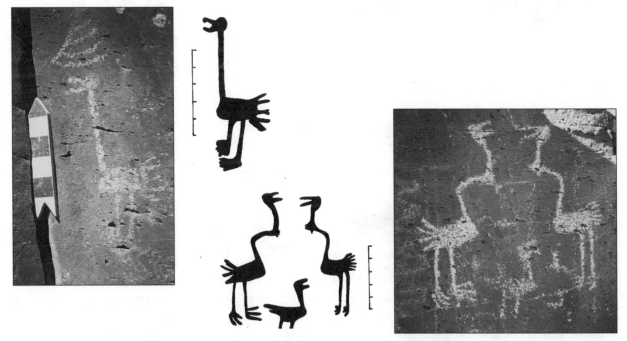

Photos 126 and 127. Petroglyphs from east/central Arizona showing cranes. The long neck is often exaggerated both in petroglyphs and ceramic illustrations.

capitation. These depictions may be illustrations of a myth or legend which has been lost in the oral traditions over the centuries. The migratory patterns of the crane are also associated with the movements of the sun and because of this cranes are important in pueblo solstice rituals (Tyler 1979).

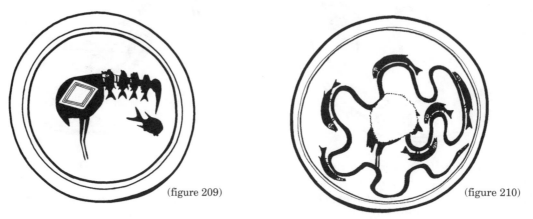

(figure 209)

(figure 210)

Figures 209 and 210. Mimbres bowls dating between A.D. 950 and A.D. 1150 showing cranes with exaggerated necks and fish (Brody 1983 and Fewkes 1924).

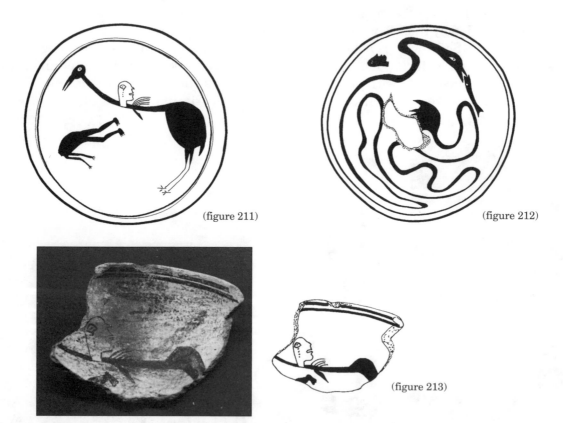

(figure 211)

(figure 212)

(figure 213)

Figures 211, 212 and 213. Mimbres ceramics dating between A.D. 950 and A.D. 1150 showing cranes and their association with decapitation. It is interesting to notice that the ceramic sherd (figure 213) exhibits exactly the design layout, number of tears and feathers as the complete bowl. This demonstrates that many of the Mimbres ceramics were indeed identical in content, execution and numerology. These vessels depict a story or legend that has been lost over the centuries (LeBlanc 1983, Brody 1983)

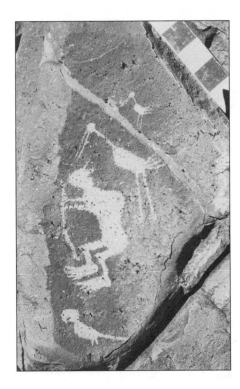

Photo 128. Petroglyph from west of Eagar, Arizona showing Kokopelli with cranes and parrots. Kokopelli is sometimes believed to be associated with parrots because of his possible identity as a long distance trader.

Turkeys

Petroglyphs that represent turkeys were not immediately identified in the rock art index of the Upper Little Colorado area. It wasn't until all of the petroglyph photographs were sorted and compared to both Mimbres ceramic depictions and the ceramic designs of the White Mountains that the turkey imagery was recognized. The minimal imagery of the prehistoric turkey usually depicts the birds with diamond-shaped heads similar to the heads portrayed on lizards. The body is also diamond-shaped and wide and the tail feathers are an equilateral triangle. Wings are represented as thin and minimal. Often within the body of the bird there will be a pattern, also within a diamond-shaped border. These patterns vary and may represent the colorful plumage of the birds. Only two animals were domesticated prehistorically in the Southwest, the turkey and the dog. For many decades researchers believed that the turkey was used principally for sacrifice during building dedications and ritualistic burials. Indeed, headless turkeys are frequently excavated as mortuary offerings. Turkey feathers were used as prayer offerings and were also split and woven into magnificent robes. Most modern pueblo cultures consider the turkey a ceremonial bird—not to be eaten. Archaeological evidence from both Casas Grandes and Mimbres ruins seems to support this, as no turkey bones have been found in the trash middens. However, more recent evidence has revealed that the birds were indeed consumed. Both headless turkey skeletons used for ceremonies and turkey bones with butcher marks indicating consumption have been excavated from Raven Site Ruins in east/central Arizona. In pueblo mythology the turkey does not represent any of the four cardinal directions but is instead believed to portray the crossing of all four directions, north, south, east and west. Turkeys are associated with death and sacrifice. The turkey is also associated with the sun and sun cults. In the mythology of the Hopi, the turkey's naked head was believed to have been singed by the sun (Stephen 1936 [Moulard 1984]).

Photos 129 (above) and 130 (left). Petroglyphs from Lyman Lake State Park in east/central Arizona depicting turkeys with the characteristic diamond-shaped head, body, and equilateral triangle representing the tail. The representation of the body of the bird often includes geometric designs and the wings are small, even minimal.

Photo 131. Ceramic Black-on-white jar neck with turkey design dating from A.D. 900 to A.D. 1200 showing a stylistic turkey with similar design elements as those found on the rock imagery of the region (White Mountain Archaeological Center Collections).

Figures 214 and 215. Mimbres bowls dating between A.D. 900 and A.D. 1150 showing turkeys. The diamond-shaped body with interior patterns and the equilateral triangle tail are common design elements (Brody 1977).

Quail

Representations of quail in the rock imagery of the Upper Little Colorado region are identified by their distinguishing top-notch. These short feathers on top of the head give the birds a comical appearance which is further enhanced by their behavior of running in line. Several of the petroglyph examples which illustrate quail include these birds in a linear series.

Photos 132 (left) and 133 (below). Petroglyphs which probably represent quail from the Upper Little Colorado region.

Quail were a game bird and an important part of the prehistoric diet. Trapping or snaring quail and other birds as well is documented on Mimbres ceramics. Quail motifs are often found on the ceramics of the Hohokam.

The mythology of the Zuni, Tewa and Tiwa includes the scaled quail and the mythology of the Hopi includes the Gambel's quail and the Montezuma quail (Moulard 1984). The modern Pima feature the quail in their mythology usually set in opposition to the coyote. The quail is seen as a mother figure.

Photo 134. Petroglyph from west of Eagar, Arizona showing an unusual anthropomorph and a quail.

(figure 216)

Figures 216 and 217. Mimbres bowls dating from A.D. 950 to A.D. 1150. Figure 216 shows a quail and the border of the bowl is executed in a design which may represent a fence. (Moulard 1984).

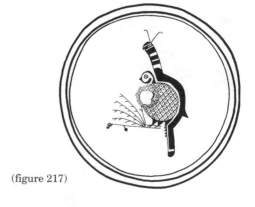

(figure 217)

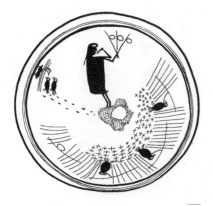

Figure 218. Mimbres bowl dating from A.D. 950 to A.D. 1150 showing fencing and snaring of ground birds. Notice that the man setting the snares is performing a blessing or prayer upon the three snares that he is holding (Brody 1977).

Eagles, Birds of Prey, Thunderbirds

Birds of prey are identified in the rock imagery of the Southwest by their predominant wings and talons. They are principally identified in pueblo mythology with the sun, knife wing, bow of the skies, i.e., the rainbow and lightning arrows and the ability to live in the realm of the gods above, to literally pass through the hole in the sky to the upper regions. Thunderbirds hold a similar identity, but they are more specifically involved with the bringing of rain. They are also associated with rainbows, thunder, clouds and lightning. Thunderbirds are usually depicted with cloud wings which they clap together to produce thunder.

Photo 135. Petroglyph from north of Raven Site Ruins in east/central Arizona showing a bird of prey. Large wings and extended talons help identify these predators that swoop down from the sky.

Photos 136 (left) and 137 (right). Ceramic bowls dating from A.D. 1325 to A.D. 1400 showing Thunderbirds. Photo 136 illustrates the stylized bird with the knife edged wings and Photo 137 shows the bird with strong rain-bringing attributes including cloud wings and a trailing rain streamer (Cunkle 1993, White Mountain Archaeological Centers Collections).

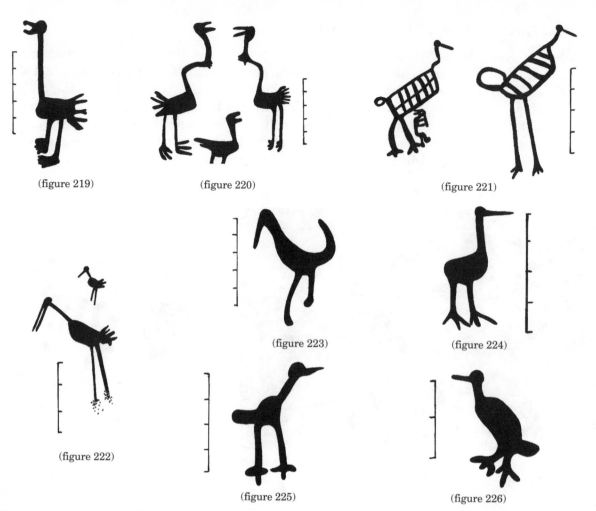

Figures 219-226. Petroglyphs illustrating cranes and water fowl from the Upper Little Colorado region.

Figures 227 & 228. Petroglyphs from the Upper Little Colorado River area showing quail.

Figures 229-231. Petroglyphs from the Upper Little Colorado River area showing turkeys.

(figure 232)

(figure 233)

Figures 232-233. Petroglyphs from the Upper Little Colorado River area showing turkeys.

(figure 234)

(figure 235)

(figure 236)

(figure 237)

Figures 234-237. Petroglyphs from the Upper Little Colorado River area showing parrots.

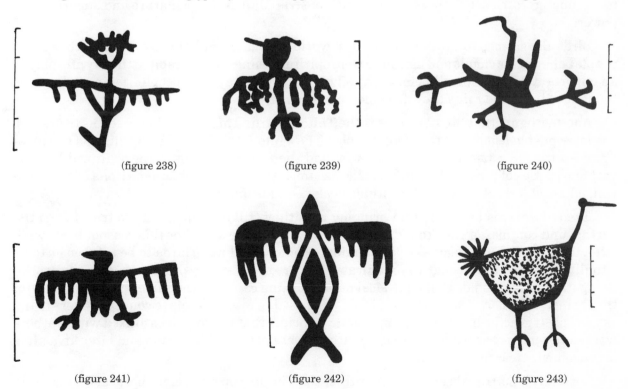

(figure 238)

(figure 239)

(figure 240)

(figure 241)

(figure 242)

(figure 243)

Figures 238-243. Petroglyphs from the Upper Little Colorado region in east/central Arizona showing birds and possible bird forms. Bird imagery is very abundant and accounts for a large percentage of the recorded petroglyph index.

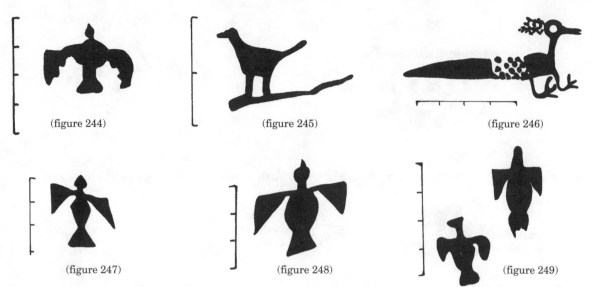

Figures 244-249. *Petroglyphs from the Upper Little Colorado region in east/central Arizona showing birds and possible bird forms.*

RITUAL ASPECTS OF BIRDS

What people have not looked to the gliding and soaring of birds without sensing the graceful spirit of these feathered beings? By the very fact that birds could easily do something that was, to our ancestors, clearly impossible, they demonstrated their divine nature and supernatural power.

Birds also seemed to be a part of the spirit world associated with the sky. Many of the pueblo people believed the clouds and lightning were spiritual beings who inhabited the sky and played an important part in the well-being of the physical world. The "cloud people", for instance, were thought to bring the rains they depended upon so heavily.

Another figure that brought rains is the Thunderbird. This mythic being seems to predate the later pueblo legends of the cloud people. The Thunderbird, like Kokopelli, was a central figure in the older pantheon of deities who had their origins in the preagricultural hunter-gather societies of the Southwest. It can be assumed the characteristic depictions of the open-winged Thunderbird were used in rituals designed to bring rains.

Even after birds lost their rain-bringing role, they still had the ability to travel from the earthbound confines of the ground to the spirit world of the sky. For this reason, birds were often used to send messages skyward. Tribal people would raise birds to be set free or to be ritually killed so they could communicate, in person or spirit, prayers to the sky world. Sympathetic magic holds that a physical part of a being can have the same spiritual powers of that being. Therefore, the feathers of birds were used in many rituals to convey prayers to the sky world. It is according to this sympathetic principle that prayer sticks affixed with feathers worked to send messages to the gods. Feathers were also used in shrine and later kiva altar arrangements to convey prayer.

Petroglyph portrayals of birds other than the Thunderbird were, in most cases, meant to communicate the shaman's ritual prayers to the spirit world. At the end of a ritual request the shaman would draw upon the bird image to send those prayers skyward.

CENTIPEDES

One image that appears in great abundance in the Upper Little Colorado area of east/central Arizona is the centipede. Dozens of depictions have been discovered. Many of these are very realistic, showing not only the multiple legs but also the head with antennae and the posterior appendages. There seems to be more centipede petroglyphs in the Upper Little Colorado region than are found in other petroglyph areas of the greater Southwest.

The multiple legs of these centipede petroglyphs are believed to represent the different levels of emergence or existence. Many researchers count the legs and associate this numerology with the various creation myths of the pueblo people (Boma Johnson personal communique). Many petroglyph panels illustrate anthropomorphs in prayer stance in association with what appears to be either a centipede or a ladder. In pueblo mythology the people climbed up from the underworld on a reed or ladder. The centipede's multiple legs are believed to represent the single pole ladder and this myriapod's subterranean existence is believed to be associated with the underworld.

Modern Native Americans from both the Hopi and Zuni tribes when queried about the nature of these petroglyphs will become uncomfortable and silent, offering no explanation whatsoever. This is probably because the centipede is believed to represent the underworld or realm of the dead. Because of the large numbers of centipede depictions that were created prehistorically this taboo probably did not exist during the execution of the glyphs. Fear of the dead is a very recent addition to Indian philosophy. Centipede petroglyphs that are located in

Photos 138 and 139. Centipede petroglyphs found north of Raven Site Ruins on the Upper Little Colorado River in east/central Arizona. Photo 138 (left) is a very realistic depiction with nine legs on either side of the body. The number nine is associated with the nine levels of emergence/existence by some researchers. Other researchers associated the numbers seven or five with the various levels of emergence/existence in pueblo thought. Photo 139 (right) is a centipede petroglyph adjacent to an elaborate shrine site.

areas which were later used by more modern Indian groups are often rubbed out or otherwise changed by the inhabitants of the area.

Depictions of centipedes are also frequently found on prehistoric ceramics. They often decorate ladle handles or the exteriors of bowls.

One remarkable ceramic depiction illustrates an anthropomorph who has been shot with an arrow. His internal organs/life breath/whirlwind are hanging out on the ground. His legs are splayed upwards indicating his eminent passage into another level of existence (legs are not necessary during level changes or vortex floating) and in his hand he is holding a giant centipede. The centipede in this depiction probably represents the single pole ladder, the underworld and/or the several levels of emergence/existence symbolized by the multiple legs.

Photo 140. Centipede petroglyph from Casa Malpais Ruin near Springerville, Arizona. Modern Native informants became very uncomfortable when queried about the nature of this petroglyph. Centipedes are associated with the underworld or realm of the dead.

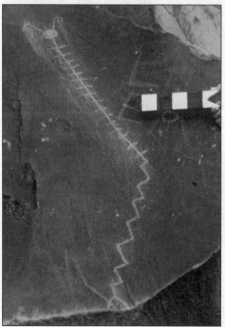

Photo 141. Large centipede petroglyph north of Raven Site Ruins, Arizona. Notice that the head and upper body areas have suffered some obliteration which occurred long after the glyph was created. This attempt to rub out the image may have been made by a more modern Native American who felt that the image was taboo.

Photo 142. Centipede petroglyph from east / central Arizona. This mega-legged depiction is very high up on a canyon wall that is also covered with footprints, tracks and other symbols.

Photo 143. Possible centipede petroglyph north of Raven Site Ruins in east / central, Arizona. This example lacks the distinctive head or posterior appendages.

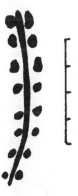

Photo 144. Possible centipede petroglyph found near a shrine site in east / central Arizona. Many of these petroglyphs have either eight or nine legs depicted on either side of the body.

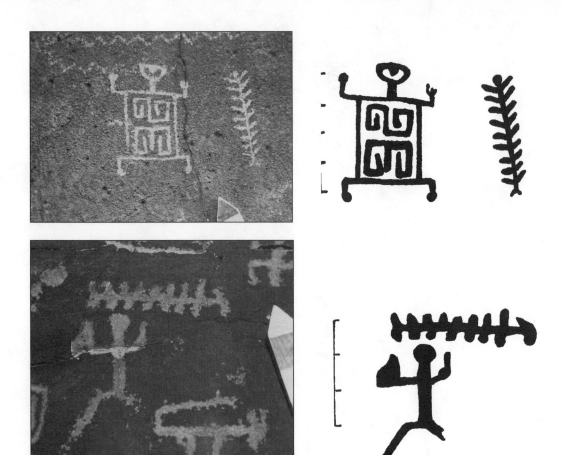

Photos 145 and 146. Petroglyphs from shrine sites in east/central Arizona showing anthropomorphs in a prayer/blessing stance with emergence symbols, emergence reeds or possible centipede representations. Photo 145 illustrates a full-bodied anthropomorph in prayer/blessing stance with the emergence ladder/reed/centipede and a wavy horizontal surface above. This depiction displays all of the creation myth symbolism.

Figure 250. Mimbres Black-on-white ceramic bowl dating between A.D. 950 and A.D. 1150 showing a dying anthropomorph holding a centipede. The depiction illustrates several concepts. This fantastic bowl was looted in the early 1960's, sold and resold many times. Its whereabouts today is unknown.

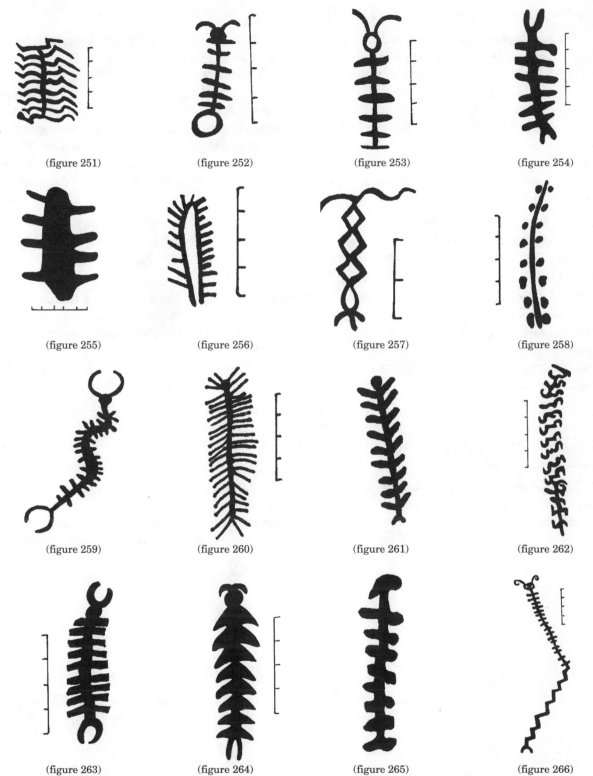

(figure 251)   (figure 252)   (figure 253)   (figure 254)

(figure 255)   (figure 256)   (figure 257)   (figure 258)

(figure 259)   (figure 260)   (figure 261)   (figure 262)

(figure 263)   (figure 264)   (figure 265)   (figure 266)

Figures 251-266. Various centipede petroglyphs from the Upper Little Colorado region in east/central Arizona. The centipede frequently appears in the rock imagery of the district and seems to be almost overly represented as compared to other images of the Southwest. The centipede is associated with the underworld and can represent the emergence ladder from the pueblo creation myths.

RITUAL ASPECTS OF CENTIPEDES

The centipede is one of the more impressive insects of the Southwest. They can be a writhing copper mass of legs and poisonous pincers over 25cm long. Centipedes are dwellers of the underworld. They are seldom seen unless you overturn rocks or dig into the earth. As a symbol of the underworld, centipedes were closely associated with the spirit world and, in more recent times, with death. Contemporary tribal sources are reluctant to volunteer any information about centipedes. They have become a taboo subject. The rules governing association with spiritual matters is what determines taboo. Centipedes are taboo precisely because they were and still are regarded as powerful sources of spiritual energy. Laypeople were not meant to be exposed to such power. Only the shaman was qualified to deal with this potentially dangerous source of spiritual force.

It is because centipedes were potent sources of power that we find so many of them in petroglyph depictions. Unlike most animals, centipedes were thought to regularly travel to the underworld. They were not limited to the physical world. In this way they are similar to snakes, though lacking the rebirthing qualities of their lizard brethren.

Because centipedes were believed to travel back and forth from the spirit world to the earth, they also posed a danger of spiritual contamination. Because all illness had a spiritual source, spiritual forces could be very dangerous to the living. It is this threat that made the centipede dangerous as it was thought capable of bringing dangers directly from the spirit world. This type of contamination is similar to the contemporary Navajo illness of "spirit sickness" that people acquire by handling the objects of the dead.

A second symbolic meaning of centipedes, a component of their ritual use, was their representation of levels of emergence. The spiritually transcendent nature of centipedes made them natural sources of transformational energy. Transformative energy was used by the shaman to transform a particular individual through rites of passage such as puberty rituals.

What many interpret as centipede depictions were in fact pole ladders. It is fortunate that the ladder was also a symbol of emergence and transitional levels. The shamans of Central Asia use ladders in rituals of transformation and emergence into the spirit world. The ancient shamans of the Southwest may have used petroglyph ladder depictions for similar rituals.

INSECT FORMS AND HUMAN-INSECT COMBINATIONS

Insect forms and human combinations with insect qualities are frequently encountered in the rock imagery of the Southwest. Many of the petroglyphs from the Upper Little Colorado River area illustrate insects that are easy to recognize. Realistic butterflies, pond skates and stylized dragonflies can be quickly identified.

However, most of the insect petroglyphs are so generic that the specific family of insect represented cannot be ascertained. Simple stick figures with six legs and a head probably represent an insect. What these simple insect figures represented to the prehistoric peoples who pecked out the glyphs is a matter of speculation. A study of the mythology of the pueblo peoples will suggest clues to the nature of various insects and the roles they played in prehistoric life ways and beliefs.

The butterfly, for example, is believed to be associated with the squash blossom (flowers in general) and fertility. All analysis of symbols and rock imagery depictions should be approached on at least two levels, the physical and the spiritual. The butterfly as associated with fertility is not just a symbol on the physical level, pollinating plants and promoting pregnancy, but also on a spiritual level making one ready/fertile to receive a vision or a higher spiritual awareness. The flight pattern or "flitting" of the butterfly is interpreted by modern Native Americans to be representational of the flight of those who have entered the spirit world.

"They (butterflies) were treated with affection and were thought of as the returning spirits of the dead." (Burland and Forman 1975).

Very often a human form will be combined with insect qualities, usually antennae or multiple legs. This combination is most frequently encountered on petroglyphs representing Kokopelli. Kokopelli's humpback is often defined as an insect form, i.e., the katydid and locust that buzz and sing in the summer as Kokopelli uses the music of his famous flute. The locust is a patron of the Hopi Flute Society as is the desert robber fly (Parsons 1938 and Renaud 1948). Like Kokopelli, the desert robber fly is famous for its vigorous copulation. The addition of insect antennae is also frequent in Kokopelli depictions.

Dragonflies are often represented as petroglyphs and stylized on ceramics. They are basically interpreted as a water symbol. Pueblo mythology abounds with stories of dragonflies or "batolatci" bringing the rains in time of famine.

"The dragonflies have always been held in great veneration by the Moki (Hopi) and their ancestors, as they have been often sent by Oman to reopen springs which Muingwa had destroyed and to confer other benefits upon the people" (Mallery 1893 and Wallace 1986 [Patterson 1992]).

The pond skate is also associated with water and water signs. This insect when at rest on the surface of the water spreads four of its six legs in four directions and is believed to be associated with the four cardinal directions in pueblo mythology.

Many petroglyphs illustrate insect forms that cannot be specifically identified by species or associated with known mythology. The frequent addition of antennae to generic anthropomorphic figures other than just Kokopelli suggests that insect qualities and characteristics played a larger role in prehistoric thought than can be currently elucidated.

Photo 147. Petroglyph from north of Raven Site Ruins, east / central Arizona showing a six-legged insect or scorpion form with tail.

Figure 267. Mimbres vessel dating from A.D. 950 to A.D. 1150 showing two scorpions. Mimbres vessels frequently illustrate scorpions and insects and anthropomorphs with insect characteristics (Brody 1977).

Photo 148. Petroglyph from north of St. Johns, Arizona showing figure with insect qualities including six legs, tail, and antennae or pincers.

Photo 149. Petroglyph from south of Holbrook, Arizona showing a six-legged insect with a long neck and head. These stick figure insects are difficult to identify as to specific species.

Photo 150. Petroglyph from north of St. Johns showing the generic six-legged insect form.

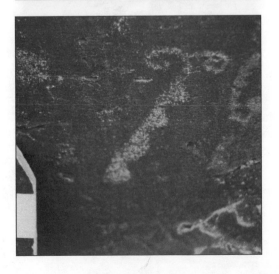

Photo 151. Insect petroglyph from Eagar, Arizona. This depiction could represent a caterpillar which suggests metamorphosis or change from one form to another, or the spiritual transition from one form to another.

Photo 152. Butterfly petroglyph from south of Holbrook, Arizona. Butterflies are associated with fertility both on the physical level of reproduction and the spiritual level of receptivity. Notice the vandalism to the left of the arrow. This malicious attempt to remove the glyph destroyed the symbols that were associated with the butterfly depiction.

Figure 268. Petroglyph from the Hopi area in northern Arizona. (Mallery 1893 and Wallace 1986 [Patterson 1992])

Figure 269. Petroglyph from Picacho Mountain, Arizona showing butterfly depictions. Several Hopi clans identify with the butterfly symbol. (Mallery 1893 and Wallace 1986 [Patterson 1992]).

Figure 270. Polacca Polychrome jar dating A.D. 1890 to A.D. 1900 showing dragonflies or "batolatci". In pueblo mythology the dragonflies were sent to reopen springs and bestow benefits to the people (Stephen 1890 [Patterson 1994]).

Figure 271. This figure is displayed on a Hopi pottery jar from the 19th century and has been erroneously identified as a butterfly. This depiction is graphic enough to identify the specific family of insect. It is, in fact, a hawk moth from the family Sphingidae and not a butterfly. The flitting flight pattern of the butterfly is believed to represent the flight of the spirits. The flight pattern of this moth resembles that of a hummingbird. It is very aggressive and direct. (Stephen 1890 [Patterson 1994]).

Photo 153. *Pinedale Black-on-red jar dating between A.D. 1275 to A.D. 1325 with butterfly symbols. (White Mountain Archaeological Centers Collections.)*

Figure 272. *Sikyatki Polychrome jar with six butterflies. (Fewkes 1895)*

Figure 273. *Stylized dragonflies on San Bernardo Polychrome jar dating A.D. 1625 to A.D. 1680. (Stephen 1890 [Patterson 1994]).*

Figure 274. *Dragonflies from kiva murals, Kawaika-a and Awatovi Ruins. (Smith 1952 [Cole 1992]).*

Photo 154. Petroglyph from north of Raven Site Ruins in east/central Arizona showing Kokopelli with insect antennae.

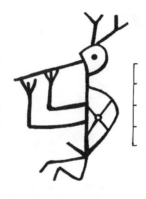

Photo 155. Petroglyph from north of St. Johns, Arizona showing a Kokopelli with insect antennae.

Photo 156. Petroglyph from north of Raven Site Ruins showing two figures with insect attributes.

(figure 275) (figure 276) (figure 277) (figure 278)

Insects

(figure 279) (figure 280) (figure 281)

Anthropomorphs with insect characteristics.

(figure 282) (figure 283) (figure 284)

Caterpillar *Kokopellis with insect attributes*

Figures 275-284. Petroglyphs from the Upper Little Colorado River area showing insects and anthropomorphs with insect attributes.

Figure 285. *Mimbres Classic Black-on-white bowl depicting Native Americans collecting locusts from bushes. The Hopi collected locusts and impaled them on sticks for roasting. Instead of the locusts bringing famine by destroying crops they were welcomed as a tasty treat (Kabotie 1982) (Figure from Brody/Scott/LeBlanc 1983).*

Figure 286. *Classic Mimbres bowl dating from A.D. 950 to A.D. 1150 showing butterfly and staff. These staff depictions often have strong fertility elements. The butterfly/moth is also a fertility sign. (Leblanc 1983).*

Figure 287. *Classic Mimbres bowl showing mirrored pond skate. The four large legs of the pond skate are believed to represent the four directions. (LeBlanc 1983).*

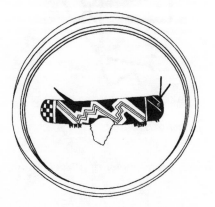

Figure 288. *Mimbres Black-on-white bowl with caterpillar. The caterpillar probably represents metamorphosis or change from one form to another (Brody 1977).*

RITUAL ASPECTS OF INSECTS

Insects are ever present beings, yet are almost oblivious to us as they go about the business of living. They are very connected to the cycles of nature. When the rains come in the summer, so too come the flies, the beetles, and the mosquitos. At the height of summer, the cicadas sing in the valleys, the dragonflies dart through the air, and butterflies flutter through the desert blooms. When the snows come to the high country, the insects disappear. The only place you find insects in the winter is in the earth. Ants are still deep in their dens, and the dark ground, the underworld, plays host to others.

Because insects were perceived to be transitory beings who disappeared into the underworld, they embodied their own spiritual powers that had their origins in the spiritual underworld. The spiritual energy of the underworld was focused through each insect species and transmuted into that insect's own spiritual force.

Petroglyphs of a particular insect were created in an effort to control the mythically assigned power of that insect. Insects were not a food staple. Therefore, they were not a component of hunt-magic. Insect images were used for their particular powers. For example, dragonflies were used to evoke the rains with which they are associated.

According to the contemporary pueblo tribes, a number of insects and their associated powers were the provence of particular clans. These clans adopted particular rituals from the shaman as pueblo culture developed. With the rituals, the clans also inherited associated beings, such as insects. Hence, we have insects associated with particular clans such as the Zuni Red Ant Society.

Once a clan or society of the tribe "had the rights" to a particular insect and its rituals, it was the clan's responsibility to employ the powers of those rituals when needed. The Zuni used the symbolic sting of the ant to help them defeat their enemies in war.

Mimbres bowl. A.D. 1050. This bowl depicts butterflies and an insect-like anthropomorph. (Brody 1977)

LIZARD AND FROG FORMS

Many petroglyph depictions are difficult to definitively distinguish between what is indeed a lizard and what is a man. Some of this ambiguity was conscious on the part of the prehistoric petroglyph artist and some is simply a confusion over what is a tail and what is a penis. According to pueblo mythology, before men emerged to this level of existence, the people were not complete, not fully formed. They had tails and other primitive features such as webbed feet. There is some variation between the different pueblo groups mythology.

The Zuni identify these figures as "...the way the Zuni looked at the time of the beginning...in the fourth underworld...when we still had tails." (Young 1988)

Many of the petroglyphs represented humankind before or during this emergence to the fourth (or fifth) level of existence. Therefore, many of the rock imagery panels include men with lizard features.

"When the people reached this surface after having traveled through the four underworlds, they were dazzled by the light of the sun and were made human by the Twins (Twin War Gods). They were washed, their tails were cut off, their webbed digits were separated and the genitals were removed from the tops of their heads. They were also hardened or finished in the same fire with which the Twins hardened the soft surface of the earth." (Young 1988 [Patterson 1992]).

Photo 157. Petroglyph from south of Holbrook, Arizona showing a lizard or frog with long tail and rounded belly in the classic "prayer" stance. Notice the tail has been separated from the body or cut off as in the creation myth of the pueblo people.

Photo 158. Petroglyph from south of Holbrook, Arizona exhibiting two lizard forms.

Petroglyphs abound of male anthropomorphs which include representations of the genitals. Lizards, frogs, or men before emergence to this level can be identified by the more distinctive lizard/frog features such as a rounded belly, very long tail, and three toes. This three-toed representation has also been identified as a shamanistic feature probably stemming from the mythology of webbed feet.

In the Upper Little Colorado area all but one of the lizard representations discovered so far in rock imagery also display the "prayer" stance, that is, both arms and hands raised upwards. This prayer stance is very common with lizard, frog and anthropomorphic representations.

Along the Little Colorado River north of Raven Site Ruins there are several petroglyphs that clearly represent horned toads or horned lizards. The horned toad is also a frequent illustration on Hohokam ceramics and can occasionally be found on Mimbres and White Mountain Redware vessels. The horned toad probably represents a more specific concept than the basic emergence myth reiterated by the Hopi and Zuni.

Photo 159. Petroglyph from south of Holbrook, Arizona showing two lizards or anthropomorphs with pre-emergence features including tails and three toes. The figure on the right exhibits the legs splayed upwards which is often an indication of floating or vortex travel from one level of existence / emergence to another.

Photo 160. Petroglyph from north of Raven Site Ruins in east / central Arizona displaying a lizard or frog form complete with rounded belly, short tail or penis and three toes and prayer stance.

Figure 289. Mimbres Black-on-white bowl A.D. 950 to A.D. 1150 illustrating the mythological transition from a lizard form to man. (LeBlanc 1983).

Photo 161. Petroglyph from north of Raven Site Ruins showing two distinctive horned toad forms both demonstrating the prayer stance. This petroglyph has been pecked into the patina and then fine scratch lines have been added to enhance the depiction.

Photo 162. Petroglyph from north of Raven Site Ruins in east / central Arizona showing a horned toad both pecked and scratched into the patina.

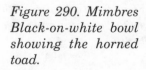

Figure 290. Mimbres Black-on-white bowl showing the horned toad.

Figure 291 depicts two horned toad figures from Hohokam ceramics. (Brody 1983 and Haury 1978).

Figures 292, 293 and 294. Mimbres Black-on-white bowls dating from A.D. 950 to A.D. 1150 showing lizards. (Brody 1983 and Fewkes 1923).

Figures 295, 296 and 297. Mimbres Black-on-white bowls dating from A.D. 950 to A.D. 1150 showing frogs. These are often associated with other water symbols. (Brody 1977, LeBlanc 1983 and Fewkes 1923)

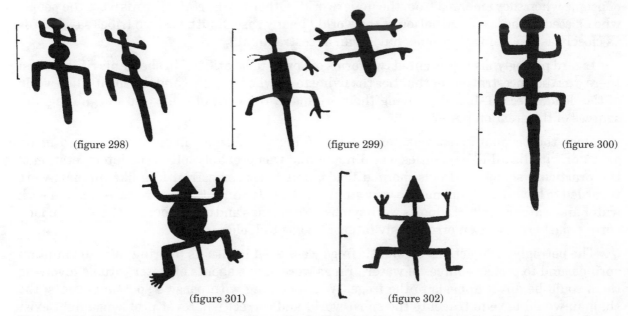

(figure 298)

(figure 299)

(figure 300)

(figure 301)

(figure 302)

Figures 298-302. Petroglyphs from the Upper Little Colorado River area showing lizard and frog forms. Lizards are associated with the pueblo creation myth and frogs are often associated with other water symbols and transition or metamorphosis from one form to another.

(figure 303)   (figure 304)   (figure 305)

(figure 306)   (figure 307)

Figures 303-307. Petroglyphs from the Upper Little Colorado River area showing lizard and frog forms.

RITUAL ASPECTS OF LIZARDS AND FROGS

Most pueblo myths saw lizards as very close relations to people, and representing the form of people when they emerged from the underworld. Other myths claim lizards were the people who existed in the last incarnation of the world. In any case, Southwestern tribes saw lizards as closely associated with people, having an ancestral quality.

Lizard petroglyphs represented two forms of power to be utilized in shamanic ritual. First there was the ancestral power that ties the living to all who have died and the spirit-filled world of the dead. Second, lizards, having their origins in the time of the world's beginning, are sources of the creation power.

Once the original artist was gone, determining whether an image was a lizard or an ancestor with lizard-like qualities was difficult and was probably left to the interpretation of the practicing shaman. Toads, horned toads, and other terrestrial frog-like animals were regarded to have a spiritual nature very similar to lizards. Aquatic frogs were associated with water and water rituals. Tadpoles were symbolic of springs and other sources of water. In fact, spring markers are often erroneously interpreted as tadpoles.

The petroglyph depictions of aquatic frogs were used in rituals to bring rain, to maintain springs, and to protect sources of water. Frogs were active agents of water; rituals involving them could be direct appeals to the frogs. When dealing with passive spiritual agents, the shaman would have to travel to the spirit world and correct whatever problems might exist himself. Active agents such as frogs, lizards and other animals were appealed to and counted on to solve problems in the spirit world.

SERPENTS

Images of serpents are common throughout the rock imagery of the Southwest. Many possible serpent representations are indistinguishable from images that may depict rivers, or mountain ranges or trails. Those that clearly illustrate serpents include the head and sometimes the tongue and rattle tail. Serpents in pueblo mythology are water symbols and underworld figures. Snakes reside near springs and they are associated with underground water. In many cases the ambiguity between the image of the serpent and the image of a river may be due to a combined meaning associated with the similar appearance of the two and the serpent's fraternity with other water elements.

The serpent is an earthbound figure, the most elemental of animals, limbless, belly to the ground and symbolic of humankind's limitations, failings, and weaknesses. Throughout the mythology of the world the serpent plays this role.

However, add wings to the serpent or plumes or feathers, and the serpent represents humankind's ability to transcend earthly limitations, the lowly serpent becomes magical, empowered with flight. Plumed serpents and dragons represent humankind's ability to spiritually rise above earthly handicaps and be like the gods.

The plumed serpent is prevalent in pueblo thought and Mesoamerican mythology. Stone carvings that embellish doorways illustrating the plumed serpent date as early as 300 B.C.

The image of the plumed serpent is later associated with the Toltec god Quetzalcoatl and legends describe him as a bearded white man who taught the arts, writing, the calendar and law. Upon Quetzalcoatl's death he ascended into heaven and became the morning star which is symbolized by the outlined or double outlined cross.

Hopi mythology identifies the plumed serpent as "Palulukon", the water serpent. To the Zuni he was "Kolowisi", the great horned serpent and guardian of springs (Grant 1967).

Figure 308. Mimbres bowl dating from A.D. 950 to A.D. 1150 showing a rattlesnake and four young. Diamond patterns or linked diamond imagery associated with certain rattlesnakes is a symbol that is identified with serpents and the right of passage ceremony of young girls. The large rattlesnake illustrated on this bowl displays a grid dot pattern that is one of the symbols for corn, and the hour glass symbol which many researchers believe is a water or water gourd symbol. The forked tongue is also identified as a lightning symbol (Brody 1977).

Figure 309. Mimbres bowl dating from A.D. 950 to A.D. 1150 showing a plumed / horned serpent with a fishtail. The plumed or horned serpent is identified by both the Hopi and Zuni as the guardian of underground springs. The fishtail adds still another water element to the serpent imagery (Brody 1977).

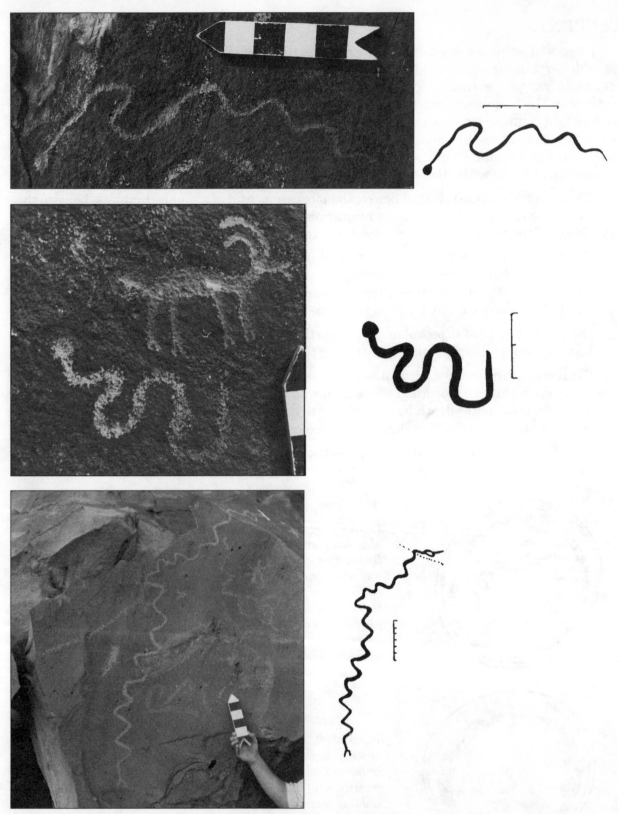

Photos 163, 164 and 165. Petroglyphs from the Upper Little Colorado region that represent serpents. Serpents are associated with other water elements: rivers, lightning and underground springs.

Figure 310. Mimbres bowl dating between A.D. 950 and A.D. 1150 showing a plumed / horned serpent with turtles. Again the grid dot "corn" pattern is seen on the head of the serpent and the turtle identifies the serpent with other water elements (Fewkes 1914).

Figure 311. Mimbres Black-on-white bowl dating from A.D. 950 to A.D. 1150 showing two figures, one being decapitated with a flint knife and the other performing the ceremony, wearing a plumed or horned serpent costume. This bowl may be illustrating a legend of the Warrior Twins who fooled the gods by feigning death (Brody 1977).

RITUAL ASPECTS OF SERPENTS

Snakes are common in the Southwest and, in the form of the rattlesnake, are respected. They were regarded as transitory figures bound to earth, who descended into the underworld and, in the form of lightning, could live as powerful beings in the sky. Snakes were also symbols of rebirth (another form of transition), accomplished every time the snake shed its skin, emerging from the process renewed.

As transitory, rebirthing beings, the snake was a powerful source of transitional spiritual energy that could be used through petroglyphs. Like centipedes, snake symbols could encourage the growth or transition of individuals from one stage of being to another. The serpent power could bring about a rebirth of being, leaving behind the old "skin" of self.

As lightning symbols, the sky serpent brought a change in weather. As the thunderclouds rolled in over the canyons, the shaman saw the bolting sky serpents come to earth with the rains behind them. Thus, lightning serpents could be powerful tools to bring rain.

Serpents were further associated with water because of their presence near springs and rivers. This association has continued in the culture of the contemporary pueblo tribes. In addition to rain rituals, serpents may have been used in rituals that maintained the vitality of springs and rivers.

Healing

Just over the rise Wind Feather could see the emerald green of the spring's ravine. Tall grasses, willows, and reeds moved in the strong winds that marked the end of winter and the beginning of spring.

Wind Feather made her way through the soggy earth and thick grasses until she found the head of the spring. A small shallow pool formed at the base of a sheer rock wall. From under a low ledge of the wall, a slow stream of pure water emerged from the dark stone.

Wind Feather set her cloth bag down in the grass and extracted a hoe-shaped hand tool. She set her feet in the cool, muddy water and began to dig a deep basin in the soft mud of the pool. When she finished, she lay back in the grass and waited for the flow of the stream to clear the newly-deepened pool.

From the spring bank, Wind Feather could see the spiral and wavy lines of the spring markers carved upon a lone pillar of stone standing in the field of green. The spring petroglyphs reinforced the power and the flow of the spring. The marks maintained a permanent presence of spring energy. Even when the spring dried up, as it did from time to time, the spirit would never forget that the spring belonged there.

Wind Feather watched the dragonflies chase one another through the winds and the sunshine as she soaked up the soothing power of the spring.

When the pool cleared, Wind Feather pulled her canteen from her bag and carefully filled it with spring water. She was careful to avoid getting any dirt into the container. The water must be very pure.

Back at the pueblo a child was very sick. Snow Flint had been tending to the little boy all night. This morning the shaman asked Wind Feather to come to this place and get pure spring water. Many of the most potent healing potions used fresh spring water as a base. Wind Feather had watched Snow Flint minister to the child throughout the night. He had to be exhausted. Even she could hardly keep herself awake. But the shaman continued on and would probably work through the coming night as well. Snow Flint would enter his trance and travel through the spirit world to find the spirits harming the boy. At the same time, Wind Feather would feed the child the medicines that would strengthen his body.

With the canteen full, Wind Feather set out for the pueblo. She would relieve Snow Flint so that he could eat.

MARKERS

Interpreting or translating petroglyph depictions must be attempted with caution. A panel may have been used by many different prehistoric peoples over a period of several thousand years. The depictions on the panel were probably carved by dozens of different people many later connected only by the spacial definition of the place, the rock face itself. Many of these ancient artists may have been just as confused by earlier depictions as we are fascinated today.

Symbols and designs were placed at specific places for specific purposes. It could be argued that any site shared this "specific purpose" observation, including social and religious observations. However, here we refer to the more mundane, the need to find or locate a particular spot for a specific purpose.

These "locators" are petroglyphs with the specific function of indicating where something can be found. These mark the location of springs, caves, trails, and other petroglyph panels. The meaning of these locator petroglyphs is often clearly understandable even to modern eyes. The symbols and combination of symbols found on locator petroglyphs greatly aid in the understanding and translation of other more complex glyph combinations.

If you have any doubt that an accurate meaning can be assigned to the prehistoric symbols found on rock art or ceramics, a study of known locators is a good place to begin your investigations. The meaning of these petroglyphs has been ascertained by the location of the glyph in relation to the surrounding environment. They are prehistoric signposts. Context of the symbols is probably the single most important element to consider during translation attempts. Locators have a built-in context.

SPRING MARKERS

During the photographing and recording of the location of several petroglyph panels in east/central Arizona, it was observed that many of these sites are found in direct association with flowing freshwater springs. In each instance where springs were discovered, glyph panels were found that illustrated the spring. These spring images share several common elements of design and meaning. Because these glyphs share common glyph elements and a common purpose, i.e., to create the image of the spring and thereby the magic which sustains and regenerates the flow of water, they are among the few petroglyphs which can be translated with relative certainty.

Spring images often include the "descending/ascending" spiral with a second "wavy line" glyph touching and in direct association with the spiral. This second wavy line glyph illustrates the water from the spring running down behind the rock. The "descending" spiral is often used in association with the spring glyph images (and locators and trail markers) and it is often combined with other symbols that represent water.

Marking the image of the spring with spirals and other petroglyphs is not only a way to easily locate the water source, but is also part of the ritual life of the prehistoric people. By adding the magic of other water symbols to the rocks near the spring they honor the spring and the underground water sources and create the magic needed to ensure that the spring will continue to flow.

Many spring images include a wavy line "water" symbol that includes a round circle at the bottom. This circle is intended to represent the source of the spring, or the spring origin.

This wavy line with a circle is nearly identical to a symbol found on protohistoric ceramics created by the Hopi. This symbol has been translated by the modern Hopi as a "tadpole" or an immature frog. The tadpole as a water symbol is also associated with other water signs. The circle and wavy line combination could also be translated as a serpent. There is really no contradiction because serpents are also associated with underground water sources (Crown 1994). This tadpole/serpent symbol and the petroglyph symbol marking the springs are also identical to the modern spring markers used on the geological survey maps produced by the Department of Interior.

This spring image depiction of a spiral combined with a tadpole or representation of the spring itself requires further discussion. Spirals are frequently used as "markers" in a general way. Every time a spiral appears in combination with other symbols as a marker, researchers have attempted to translate the spiral relative to the other symbols. For example, when a spiral is combined with a bare footprint, the depiction usually marks a trail in or out of a canyon. The

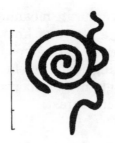

Photo 166. Spiral and wavy line petroglyph in combination creating the image of a freshwater spring. The spring is located behind the rock face. The wavy line is a water symbol and the spiral marks the spot, or "descending" water.

Photo 167. Spiral and "tadpole / serpent / spring" petroglyph which marks a strong freshwater spring along the Little Colorado River. The "tadpole / serpent / spring" marker used prehistorically is, ironically, identical to the symbol used by the Department of Interior on topography maps.

spiral part of the depiction is assumed to represent the trail itself or "ascend/descend". The spiral combined with the water symbol found at spring locations is assumed to represent the flowing or "descending" water. Spirals have also been found that mark the entrance to caves. This might suggest that the spiral is used to indicate "descending" into the cave. However, one dramatic example of spirals marking the cave entrance has been discovered along the Little Colorado River where six small spirals marked the entrance of the cave, and within the cave were six small prehistoric ceramic jars.

The common element here is that spirals "mark" locations. Even the Fajada Butte Sun Dagger Site of Chaco Canyon, New Mexico uses the spiral to mark the position of sunlight against the rock face.

Interestingly, the symbol for water is often represented on ceramic depictions as dots. The dot representation is frequently found on petroglyphs, although the meaning of these dots in petroglyph depictions is usually ascribed a meaning other than water. They are usually depicting tracks or the trail of an animal or anthropomorph.

On ceramics, the dot representations depict "falling rain" or "rain falling to the earth", i.e., water droplets. The wavy line depiction meaning water is also found on ceramic vessels, usually representing "still water" or "pond".

Figure 312. Hopi pottery design showing the tadpole which is the symbol of the Water Phratry. Tadpoles, serpents and other water symbols are often included in petroglyph panels that locate springs. (Stephen 1890).

 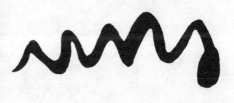

Photo 168. Serpent petroglyph from the area north of St. Johns, Arizona. The serpent is also associated with water and underground water sources.

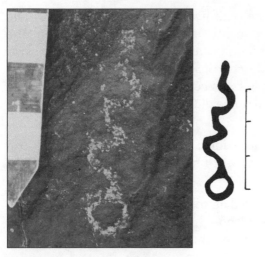

Photo 169. Spring marker petroglyph from the Upper Little Colorado River area.

Photo 170. Spring marker petroglyph from east / central Arizona with two circles and two wavy lines.

Figure 313. Tusayan Black-on-white olla design. This pattern is one of the many "still water" symbols as translated by the Hopi in 1890 (Patterson 1994).

Photo 171. Fourmile Polychrome bowl showing the "crop rows" with dots that represent "falling rain". Ceramics commonly depict rain, falling rain or water as dots (White Mountain Archaeological Center Collections).

Photo 172. Pinedale Polychrome bowl showing a circle with wavy lines representing "pond" or "still water" (Lee Jenkins personal communique). (White Mountain Archaeological Center Collections.)

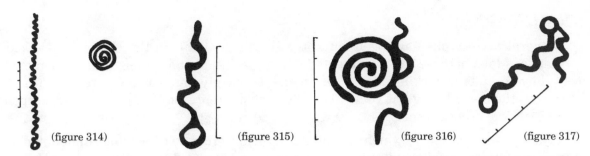

(figure 314)   (figure 315)   (figure 316)   (figure 317)

Figures 314-317. Petroglyph spring images from the Upper Little Colorado area in east / central Arizona. Common elements include: spirals which may indicate "descending" water or they may signify a more generic "X" marks the spot, wavy lines which represent water, and often attached to the wavy lines is a circle which may indicate the spring itself or create the image of the tadpole or serpent; both are well-established water symbols.

RITUAL ASPECTS OF SPRING MARKERS

On many occasions I have walked through the dry, rocky canyons of the Southwest and have found myself, quite suddenly, standing in cool green grass and the shade of willows. Little islands of green are scattered here and there in the hills, rocks, and sands of the desert. If you are lucky enough to find such a place, you will also have a good chance of finding petroglyphs or a shrine.

Like the grasses and willows, tribal people were often sustained by the springs of their land. Seeds could be sown in the spring oasis for later harvest or the spring could offer water and sustenance during a long trek. Springs could also offer spiritual sustenance.

The water from a spring was not the same as the water from a river. A river was a thing of the physical world. Though sacred, it existed entirely in the world of the living. The spring, however, emerged from the underworld, from the spirit world. Spring markers, in most cases, did not serve to inform the traveler of the spring's existence (the greenery made that obvious). Instead, spring markers were used in rituals that worked with the spiritual power of the spring. There are accounts of spring water being used in rain and agricultural rituals. This would imply a strong connection between spring water and water rituals. This makes sense from the perspective of sympathetic magic. Spring water, by nature, was connected to the spirit of all water, and was further empowered through its emergence from the underworld of spirit.

Spring water could be used as a powerful base for the healing formulas of the shaman. To drink spring water activated through the effort of the tribal shaman was to drink the fluid energy of the underworld. The shamanic rituals involved would direct the action of the underworld energy. This type of ritual would involve spring marker petroglyphs. With the spring petroglyphs, the shaman had the representative symbols of the spring's power that provided the means of using sympathetic magic.

Spring markers may have also served the purpose of reinforcing and safeguarding the spring. Many springs provide their water in a somewhat erratic manner. In some cases, they will stop for years and then flow again stronger than ever. This erratic nature of springs would encourage rituals crafted to maintain the vigorous qualities of springs. The symbol of a flowing spring has the sympathetic power to keep the spring flowing.

TRAIL MARKERS

Several petroglyphs have been found that mark the trails in the Upper Little Colorado Drainage. Many of these were not created using specific enough iconography to demonstrate that they are in fact marking a trail. Often just a squiggly line may indicate the path ahead. However, the meandering line could also just as easily represent the river, or sky serpent, or any number of other meanings.

The ever present spirals which are found in a variety of context and which undoubtedly have a variety of meanings depending upon their context are also frequently found in the correct locations that seem to imply that they are indeed marking a trail, usually up or down a canyon. In this context the spiral probably is a trail marker, using the "ascend/descend" meaning and marking the spot to climb up or climb down to get out of the canyon or wash.

Recently discovered petroglyphs in narrow canyons south of Holbrook, Arizona also display the spiral with the "ascend/descend" meaning marking trail locations which are advantageous to climb up and out or in and down along the route.

Fortunately several prehistoric people carved a more specific depiction to mark the place that was easiest for egress and ingress. At several locations along the canyon bottom and top a figure can be observed which is a combination of a bare footprint connected to a meandering line. This combination is found where it is easiest to ascend or descend the canyon walls. The actual trail that is marked including hand and foot holds in the stone is still visible. The footprint symbol is often used to indicate a trail or path and this combination of the footprint and meandering line and the location of these combinations is strong evidence of a correct contextual translation.

Figure 318. Mesoamerican trader carrying the crossroads symbol. The bare footprints indicate the two trails (Codex Ferjervary-Mayer [Patterson 1992]).

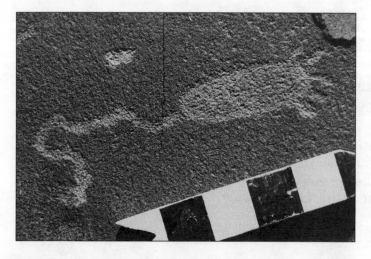

Photo 173. Petroglyph found south of Holbrook, Arizona with bare footprint connected to a short meandering line. This glyph marks the location of a short path that leads out of the canyon.

Photo 174. Petroglyph from the Upper Little Colorado area showing the footprint and the accompanying meandering line. This depiction marks a fork in the trail along the Little Colorado River.

Photo 175. Petroglyph from south of Holbrook, Arizona showing a bare footprint connected by a short line to a spiral. This petroglyph marks a place in this very vertical canyon were egress is possible. The spiral in this context indicates "ascend". The two other spirals to the left of the footprint spiral are probably similar markers and demonstrate the meaning of the spiral when used in this context.

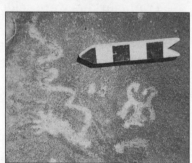

Photo 176. Petroglyph from north of Raven Site Ruins in east/central Arizona with bare footprint and meandering line which marks a trail up to the top of one of the many mesas along the Little Colorado River.

Photo 177. Petroglyph from south of Holbrook, Arizona showing bare footprints and meandering lines which indicate a trail up and out of the canyon.

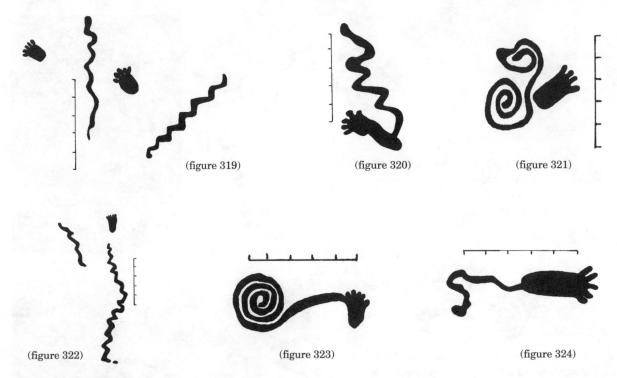

Figures 319-324. Trail markers from the Upper Little Colorado area in east/central Arizona. These locators usually include a footprint, meandering line and occasionally they are combined with the spiral.

RITUAL ASPECTS OF TRAIL MARKERS

Trail markers were seldom-used elements of shamanic ritual. Those cases in which trail markers were used in ritual are similar to the use of footprints. The shaman may have used trail markers to bless or protect travelers. Some trail markers may have been tribal warnings to trespassers that may have carried some form of magical barrier recognizable to the tribal people of a region. Or, trail markers may also have been symbolic representations of a spiritual path. In these cases the markers may have been used in shamanic rituals to bring about success in a spiritual journey.

Spiritual paths could also exist in the physical world. For the purposes of vision quests or spiritual pilgrimages, the marked trail might lead a person to a sacred destination or simply guide them during a sacred walk. In the Southwest and other parts of the world, there are documented paths that were part of religious pilgrimages. In many such cases, the walking of the path was as much a religious practice as the ritual performed at the pilgrim's destination.

Transition

Wind Feather sat on a smooth block of basalt and looked down on the pueblo in the evening light. The trees had started to change color and the fields were turning gold and brown. Dense flocks of birds drifted south through the cooling skies and, in the distance, thunderclouds played host to flashes of lightning and drifting streams of rain.

The harvests and the foraging had been very good. Jars were filled with dried maize, beans, fruit, berries and meat. The children would grow fat and the people would remain healthy this winter. Wind Feather stood and walked over to a shrine covered with freshly made petroglyphs. She placed her hand on the image of a ghost-like figure floating in the spirals of a vortex. Next to the vortex were the checker-board patterns of the night sky, the lights of the spirit world.

Wind Feather had a lot of work and responsibility ahead. A part of her felt she wasn't ready, that she had so much more to learn before she could be the shaman. The one thing that she did have, the thing that gave her courage and confidence to meet her responsibilities, was trust. She knew she had the trust of Snow Flint. She could remember the weathered, wrinkled face of her teacher, a face filled with power and capability, as he told her, "You have a special spirit; it has strength that is hidden from you, but will always be there when you need it." "Good journey, my teacher. I will miss you," she said to herself.

The death of a shaman was a difficult time. Despite her grief, she had to see to the ritual and spiritual needs of the tribe. The shaman offered stability and spiritual security. The tribe depended on the shaman for healing and protection from those forces that surrounded them in the mysterious worlds. When the apprentice had to fill that role, the tribe went through a period of vulnerability until the apprentice proved worthy. Wind Feather knew that she would have to work harder than she ever had to win the trust of her people.

Reluctantly, she left the vortex shrine and made her way toward the distant death shrine. Though she liked the thought of her teacher's spirit standing behind her, lending her strength and wisdom, she knew that she had to make him leave. She would perform the ritual of the dead in a way that would make him proud. She could see his smile as his spirit entered the spirit world.

GEOMETRICS

SPIRALS (VORTEXES)

Spirals are one of the most commonly found petroglyph depictions in the Southwest. They undoubtedly have a variety of meanings depending upon the context of the glyph.

The most frequent use of the spiral was to illustrate emergence or vortex travel from one level of existence to another. Pueblo mythology repeatedly told of the emergence from the sipapu to this world, or fourth level of existence. Upon death, the spirits again traveled through the vortex to the next level of existence, carried up (often by the eagle) through the sky window, or eye of god, into the next world.

The spiral was used in a similar way to illustrate life or life breath as the whirlwind figure. Anthropomorphs are often seen in a transitional state, in the throws of death with the life breath or whirlwind escaping from the body.

Spirals were often used in combination with other glyphs to mark trails or to mark the spot where the trail began, usually indicating an ascent upward or a descent downward. The spiral used to indicate ascent or descent is very common. This is probably why the spiral was used as a marker for solar calendars of the Southwest; i.e., the sun appeared to ascend and descend in the sky. This is also, of course, related to the spirals used in the vortex context indicating the movement, the ascending, or descending from one level to another.

In general, spirals indicated motion both on the physical level and more commonly on the spiritual level. Day to day use included marking where springs and descending water could be found and where trails began. Spiritual usage included indicating death, creation, and the spirit's travel from the body to other levels of existence.

Photo 178. Petroglyph from Lyman Lake State Park in east/central Arizona showing a well-executed spiral with a horned head, possibly indicating vortex travel or the spiritual power of the figure.

Photo 179. Petroglyph from east of Raven Site Ruins in east / central Arizona showing a spiral and wavy line which indicates the location of a fresh spring. The spiral in this context probably indicates "descending" water. The ascend and descend context of the spiral is very common.

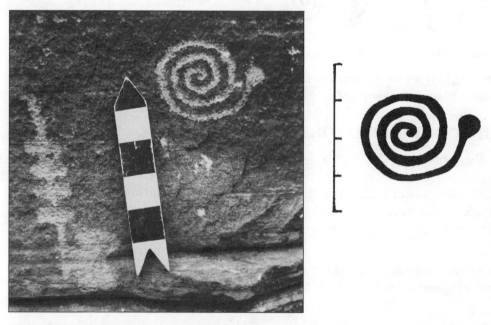

Photo 180. Petroglyph from south of Holbrook, Arizona showing a spiral with a solid circle at the end and a four ball rattle. This panel illustrates the spiral's use in the emergence, vortex context. The four circles of the rattle probably refer to this fourth world of emergence.

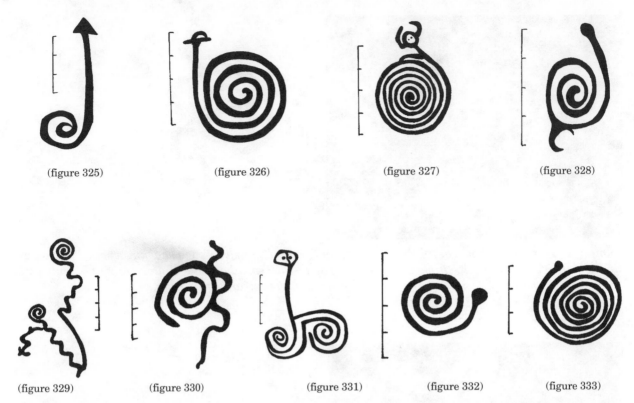

(figure 325) (figure 326) (figure 327) (figure 328)

(figure 329) (figure 330) (figure 331) (figure 332) (figure 333)

Figures 325-333. Petroglyphs from east/central Arizona showing spirals in a variety of contexts. The spiral is used principally to indicate movement on both the physical and spiritual level.

RITUAL ASPECTS OF SPIRALS (VORTEXES)

The spiral was also known as the vortex. A vortex was a doorway to an active place of transition between the physical world and the spirit world. As a vortex symbol, the spiral represented the spiritual power of transition as well as the act of transition. When a shaman was faced with a particular state of reality that needed to be changed, such as a drought, a spiral may have been used to draw upon the power of transition by activating the vortex that embodied it.

Spirals also had a variety of uses as markers with specific meanings determined by the local tribes. They may have also served as a type of boundary marker between tribes or groups within tribes.

Spiral markers have been a part of many astronomical calendar-stone arrangements. On winter and summer solstices, these spirals were pierced by knives of light marking significant seasonal events. When spirals were used to mark the regular components of the annual cycle, they, according to the shamanic prospective, reinforced the cycle of the seasons. Like the animals hunted and brought back to life via the rituals of rebirth, the seasons also went through a life-cycle. The solstice spirals most likely played a major role in shamanic rituals designed to maintain the cycle of the seasons. There are latter-day parallels to this type of ritual in the seasonal kiva ceremonies of the pueblo tribes.

OTHER GEOMETRIC DESIGNS

Many of the petroglyphs of the Southwest are designs that can be described as geometric patterns. Terraces, interlocked square spirals and curls, checkerboards and diamonds are frequent depictions. Geometric designs are not as commonly seen as are anthropomorphs and zoomorphs but they do frequently occur.

Most researchers describe these geometric elements as basket/blanket patterns or pottery designs, and indeed they do often resemble the artistry seen on baskets, blankets and pottery known from the prehistoric cultural assemblages. Many of the geometric petroglyph illustrations may contain more meaning than the simple recreation of weaving or ceramic design elements.

The checkerboard in pueblo mythology represents the Milky Way, one of the pathways for the Warrior Twins.

Opposing linked spirals are often interpreted by modern Native American informants to represent migration, or clans traveling from one place to another.

Photos 181 (top) and 182 (bottom). Petroglyphs from Lyman Lake State Park in east/central Arizona showing blanket designs. These elongated units may represent sashes. Photo 181 includes the fringe of the sash.

Linked diamonds represented several ideas including the rattlesnake, stars, and the symbol of the rites of passage for young girls into adulthood. The idea of house or phratry was often depicted by a horizontal line above which interlocked units were combined.

Hints as to the meaning of these geometric designs found on the petroglyph panels can often be discovered in a more complete context painted on the surface of prehistoric bowls and ollas. Several researchers have interpreted pottery symbols which strongly resemble the geometric elements of the petroglyphs (Patterson 1994, Fewkes 1895, Cunkle 1993, et al).

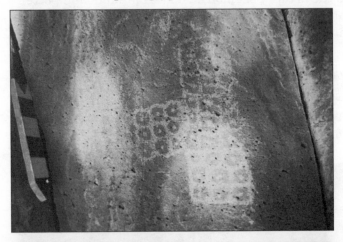

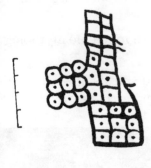

Photos 183 (above left) and 184 (left). Petroglyphs from south of Holbrook, Arizona showing possible blanket/basket or pottery designs.

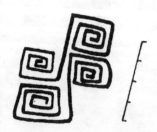

Photo 185 (left). Petroglyph from north of St. Johns, Arizona showing interlocked square spirals. Native American informants often translate these glyphs as depictions of migrations or clan movements.

Photo 186. Petroglyph from north of St. Johns, Arizona showing interlocked square spirals.

Photos 187. Petroglyph from the Upper Little Colorado region showing linked diamonds. These patterns are associated with snakes, stars, and female rites of passage.

Photo 188. Petroglyph from the Upper Little Colorado region showing linked diamonds.

Photo 189. Petroglyph from north of St. Johns, Arizona. The checkerboard is often associated with the Milky Way and is identified as a road or pathway for the Warrior Twins of pueblo mythology.

Photo 190. *The curls are identified by the Hopi as symbols that represent the female or "love locks" (Stephen 1890 [From Patterson 1994]).*

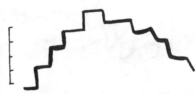

Photo 191. *Petroglyph from south of Holbrook, Arizona. The terrace is often interpreted as a cloud or a mountain.*

Photo 192. *Petroglyph from south of Holbrook, Arizona. The series of lines in this photo are usually thought to represent a counting system.*

Photo 193. *Petroglyph from north of St. Johns, Arizona. This petroglyph includes elements of two interlocked swastikas. The swastika represented the four directions.*

Photo 194. *Petroglyph from north of St. Johns, Arizona. This petroglyph resembles a ceramic symbol interpreted by Hopi informants to represent a confederated phratry house.*

Photos 195 and 196. *Petroglyphs from south of Holbrook, Arizona. Several of these symbols have been discovered and the thought is that they may have represented a specific house or clan.*

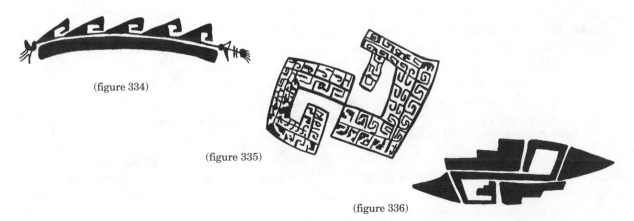

(figure 334)

(figure 335)

(figure 336)

Figures 334, 335 and 336. *These emblems are found on Sikyatki Polychrome jars dating between A.D. 1375 and A.D. 1625 and have been interpreted by the Hopi of 1890 to represent different dwelling houses or Katsina houses. (Stephen 1890 [Patterson 1994]).*

(figure 337) (figure 338) (figure 339)

(figure 340) (figure 341) (figure 342)

(figure 343) (figure 344) (figure 345)

(figure 346) (figure 347) (figure 348)

Figures 337-348. Various geometric designs from petroglyphs of the Upper Little Colorado region in east / central Arizona.

RITUAL ASPECTS OF OTHER GEOMETRIC DESIGNS

The symbolic vocabulary of the shaman must have incorporated many elements that could not be rendered in forms that would have meaning to an observer outside the shaman's own culture. Because the shaman of tribes moving into an area with pre-existing petroglyphs had their own abstract concepts, they would assign them to whatever symbols seemed most appropriate and add any that they felt were missing. Petroglyph symbols were not as rigid in their meaning as modern written language. Symbols could change their meaning to accommodate the mythic and ritualistic heritage of whatever shaman was using the depictions. For this reason it is most difficult to interpret the meaning of abstract symbols in particular, as there was no single meaning. Non-abstract depictions had more stable meanings grounded in the universal way people perceive recognizable pictures.

Many abstracts were nets and fences used to ritually contain particular spiritual beings. Others were stylized representations of rattlesnake skin, stars in the sky, or the very rare and very noteworthy occurrence of an aurora borealis. Each of these representations would have a moderately recognizable use in ritual.

The contemporary interpretations of pueblo Indians are varied and seem to be founded in later mythological elements of the Katsina religion. This is natural and to be expected as it is the nature of abstracts to change their meaning to reflect the values of the interpreter.

Part IV

Conclusion I

As this study proceeded, many aspects of the petroglyph index of the Southwest became abundantly clear. Our research teams hiked out into the field and photographed quite literally every petroglyph and pictograph that they encountered. Thousands of petroglyphs and many shrine sites were newly discovered. These photographs were then enlarged and the images traced. This process revealed many details that were otherwise obscure or even invisible. The photographs were then sorted. Anthropomorphs were piled with anthropomorphs, zoomorphs with zoomorphs, and geometrics with geometrics. As the large tables of photographs began to fill, the frequency of similar images became obvious. The pile of photographs of footprint images was many times higher than its neighbor, "animal tracks". In the zoomorphic section, the pile of photos of mountain lion petroglyph images was ten times greater than that of any other animal representation from the region.

It is not my intention here to attempt to present a frequency chart showing how one kind of image was pecked into the stone "X" amount of times more often than another type of image. Although, a frequency analysis could be a useful demonstration. However, I feel that our sample suffers major flaws. We know, in fact, that we have discovered only a tiny fraction of the total glyph assemblage in our region. It seemed that every time a team hiked out in search of petroglyphs, they would return with several new discoveries. A brief mention of the most apparent image abundances and absences is in order.

Petroglyphs of footprints which are rather uncommon throughout the Southwest are a very frequent discovery in the Upper Little Colorado River area.

Mountain lion images are by far the most common four-legged animal depicted in the east/central Arizona areas. No other zoomorphic representations came even close in number to these images. Nearly all of the animal representations depicted the larger more difficult to hunt elk, deer, bear, etc. These larger game animals required much more magic to successfully dispatch.

Birds in general are a very common glyph from our immediate research area. Many of these petroglyphs are easily identified by species.

Centipede petroglyphs outstrip even mountain lions and indeed any other single representation in frequency in central and east/central Arizona.

Small game animals such as rabbits are blatantly missing from the petroglyph index of the Southwest. The sympathetic magic required to be a successful rabbit hunter must have been quite minimal.

The representations of anthropomorphs also demonstrated some interesting frequencies. The "prayer/blessing" stance was by far the most common human depiction as were images of males as opposed to females.

Kokopelli petroglyphs were everywhere. The magic of Kokopelli and his flute must have been a very powerful force in prehistoric life. Kokopelli images began to appear around A.D. 200

and they continued to be a very frequent representation until about A.D. 1300. These fertility portraits played an important role in the agricultural societies that predominated the Southwest with the introduction of corn, beans, irrigation and the aggregation of the prehistoric pueblo communities from A.D. 200 until their fertility magic was replaced by the Katsina Cult.

Many researchers are attempting to locate petroglyphs that depict the influence of the Katsina Cult or specific Katsina images. For the most part, their efforts have been limited by the lack of these depictions within the total petroglyph index of the Southwest. It is important to remember that around the year A.D. 1300, the Katsina Cult was adopted in the pueblo communities. This involved a large portion of the population directly participating in ceremonies that created the magic that was previously the shaman's responsibility. These ceremonies were a community event and they took place, not out at the remote shrine sites where the petroglyphs were pecked into the stone, but in the central plaza of the pueblo where all could see.

The sympathetic magic of Kokopelli and the fertility images were produced by shamans for many, many centuries at the shrine sites. These pecked impressions consequentially far out-number all others. Shamanistic practices predate even the Kokopelli images. Evidence of these earlier hunter/gatherer petroglyphs are present, but again, like the Katsina images, not in large numbers.

Approaching these observations from a demographic point of view may provide a possible explanation. Hunter/gatherer societies were small, mobile extended families. Surplus people were a liability. Small groups produce fewer petroglyphic images. With the introduction of agriculture around the year A.D. 200 with corn, beans and irrigation, people began to aggregate into large stable communities. Populations increased and there was an increased need to insure the fertility of crops and people. More hands were needed to tend the fields and irrigation systems. Shamans were busy creating images that would bring the magic and insure the harvest. In the greater Southwest, this period of time is probably when the majority of petroglyph imagery was created.

Almost all of the places where petroglyphs occur in clusters are indeed shrine sites or they are associated with nearby shrines. Sometimes the shrines are obvious. Huge eclectic boulders sheltering a cave are covered with petroglyphs and nearby will be niches in the stone with offerings of shell and turquoise. Other times a small canyon is the home of thousands of petroglyphic images with no specific shrine location apparent. In these cases it is probably the canyon itself that serves as the shrine and holds the magic of the place.

When hiking the canyons it is easy to feel the omnipotence of the natural environment. The wind sings, the river laughs and the rock stands in silent testimony of a fire-born beginning. Researchers record, photograph and measure petroglyph images in the name of science. But these images created so laboriously many centuries ago have a spiritual life and power of their own, beyond any scientific recording.

James R. Cunkle

Conclusion II

Petroglyphs and the shamanic rituals that called for them may seem distant and irrelevant to the heritage of most people. But, this is far from the fact. Regardless of our culture or ethnicity, all of us can trace our lineage to a time when our ancestors held animist beliefs and practiced shamanism. These practices and the relics they left behind have played a part in greater history of all people. Petroglyphs can offer one means to further understand the common origins of human beliefs that are manifested in the practices of shamanism.

To understand the thought and belief systems underlying petroglyph rituals, we must step away from our conventional way of viewing the world. The contemporary western "worldview" is a reductionist one based on the separation of the world into different objects and events. We reduce all phenomena into its parts giving little thought to the system or interaction of the parts. We tend to discount the meaning or value of an action if we can't see a clear cause and effect. The effects of magical ritual cannot be gauged in an objective manner. Hence, we regard such rituals as the stuff of primitive peoples acting according to the dictates of superstition. But, this regard and the perceptions that produce it, blind us to the hidden qualities of the animist worldview.

To the people of animist cultures, no object, person or event was separated from the living systems of the universe. All actions and events impacted the fabric of the whole. When the ancient Americans looked at a field of growing maize they saw an extension of rains and the nurturing power of fertility deities. When they hunted game they thanked it as a friend that would be back again to feed the people. And when a loved one died, the ancients knew that he/she would continue to exist in another form in another place continuing the cycles that maintained the animistic universe. Like the spirit they felt within their own heart, the tribal ancestors felt the spirit of reality.

The animist worldview established the unquestioned perception of tangible spiritual forces. Our ancestors firmly believed that spiritual forces could be directed through techniques of ritual and sympathetic magic. Because people seem compelled by nature to harness their environment, the shaman emerged as a pervasive early practitioner of this ancient ritual craft.

The shamanic belief system served the cultures of our ancestors in numerous ways such as fostering the development of healing practices, mnemonic devices for the transition of cultural traditions, and social stability. Like other religions, shamanism brought about an individual and collective sense of security by providing a complete cosmology and the derived explanations for life's mysteries. But, most importantly, shamanism provided a means of directing the environment. Instead of being the helpless victims of circumstance or perceived malicious beings, our ancestors could respond and take ritual action. The shaman became the bulwark of ritual protection for the people while also wielding the power of spiritual action. In its essence, shamanism is about power, the power to influence those forces beyond the capabilities of tribal physical technology.

With the exception of petroglyphs, most of the particulars of prehistoric shamanism have been lost to us. However, petroglyphs, coupled with what we have learned from contemporary shamanic traditions, still speak to us of their roles in ritual action.

It is a misconception to think of petroglyphs as "rock art". When we understand the role of petroglyphs in the ritual traditions of tribal people they are cast in a new light. Petroglyphs were mediums and vessels of spiritual power that accommodated the human need to influence the forces of nature and take a hand in its own fate. Petroglyphs were the tools of the shaman's magic, his ritual technology.

This shamanic belief system strengthened, if not established, many of the archetypal images we find in contemporary culture. Whether shamanic symbols had their origins in the common perceptions of the human mind or were established by the widespread practice of shamanism, they have become an enduring part of all cultures. The religious elements of prayer, ritual and interactive deities all have their origins in prehistoric animist belief systems. The archetypes of the healer, mother, hunter, warrior, serpent and many others still resonate with our perceptions of the world. The concept of magic, though discredited by the reductionist worldview, still persists in contemporary folklore. Setting aside the vast body of contemporary religious ritual, many people still carry objects for luck or protection. Some perform elaborate rituals when they play bingo or buy lottery tickets. And others seek out the practitioners of the ancient symbolic deviational systems of tarot, astrology and rune stones to name a few. These systems still retain a wealth of complex symbols that offer multiple levels of interpretive meaning. For example, some of the potential meanings of the tarot Death card can be: a time of change, the end of a cycle, or the death of an individual. Tarot, like the other surviving magical/divination systems, is a rich body of multi-leveled symbolic meaning that permits the flexible and individualized interpretation needed for different practitioners in different social and cultural environments. Such systems are the conceptual decedents of the more ancient practice of shamanic petroglyph interpretation.

Unlike the contemporary practices of divination, the shaman was not limited to forecasting. Whereas the contemporary practitioner of divinational magic attempts to look into the future by interpreting patterns produced by his system, the shaman used the symbolic values of petroglyphs and rituals to actively influence the future.

Today we rely on our physical technology to direct the course of our future. We have separated ourselves from nature and distanced ourselves from all life but our own. We have more control over our world, but we have become isolated. We live amidst nature but not as a part of it. The animists worked from the inside, as part of the natural system, whereas we work on nature as a resource, from the outside. The worldview that supported the development of our current technology brought us impressive physical power but we have divorced the living system of life that has nurtured our species.

If you sit down in front of a petroglyph panel and take time to study it, you may get a sense of the animist worldview that precipitated its creation. If you also open your senses to the smell of wildflowers, the sounds of the wind and the animals while feeling the ground beneath you, you may bring a spark of animism alive in your mind. For a moment you may feel the forces and currents of nature flow over you, fill you and accept you as their own. In that moment, from that frame of mind, the actions of the shaman and uses of petroglyphs becomes clear.

In the end we are left with the silent presence of the petroglyphs. Perhaps a part of their magic is as the tools of the heroic human effort to stand against the dangers of life, daring to direct the forces of nature. This type of magic continues with us today in all the forms of our science and technology. But, what have we lost? Petroglyphs may reflect a deeper, more animate understanding of the world that we left behind long ago.

Markus A. Jacquemain

Bibliography

Adams, Charles E.
1991   *The Origin and Development of the Pueblo Katsina Cult.* University of Arizona Press. Tucson, AZ.

Apostolides, Alex
1984   The Story Teller Woman Panel. The Artifact 22 (2). The El Paso Archaeological Society. El Paso, TX.

Applebaum, Herbert
1987   *Perspectives in Cultural Anthropology.* State University of New York Press. New York.

Barnes, F.A.
1982   *Canyon Country Prehistoric Rock Art.* Wasatch Publishers, Inc. Salt Lake City, UT.

Beck, Peggy V., Anna Lee Walters, Nia Francisco
1992   The Sacred; Ways of Knowledge, Sources of Life. Navajo Community College Press. Tsaile, AZ.

Brody, J.J.
1977   *Mimbres Painted Pottery.* School of Am. Research. Univ. of New Mexico Press, Albuquerque, NM.
1983   *Mimbres Pottery, Ancient Art of the American Southwest.* Hudson Hills Press. New York.
1991   *Anasazi & Pueblo Painting.* School of Am. Research. Univ. of New Mexico Press. Albuquerque, NM.

Brody, J.J., Catherine J. Scott, Steven A. LeBlanc
1983   *Mimbres Pottery Ancient Art of the American Southwest.* Hudson Hills Press. New York.

Burland, Cottie A., and Werner Forman
1975   *Feathered Serpent and Smoking Mirror.* G.P. Putnam's and Sons. New York.

Campbell, Joseph
1988   *The Power of Myth.* Anchor Books. Doubleday Dell Publishing Group, Inc. New York.

Cole, Sally J.
1990   *Legacy on Stone; Rock Art of the Colorado Plateau and Four Corners Region.* Johnson Books. Boulder, CO.
1992   *Katsina Iconography in Homol'ovi Rock Art, Central Little Colorado River Valley, Arizona.* Arizona Archaeological Society. Phoenix, AZ.

Corbusier, William H.
1886   *The Apache-Yumas and Apache-Mojaves.* American Antiquarian, September 1886. Jameson and Morse. Chicago.

Cordell, Linda S.
1984   *Prehistory of the Southwest.* Dept of Anthropology, Univ. of New Mexico, Albuquerque, NM. and Academic Press, Inc. New York.

Crown, Patricia L.
1994   *Ceramics and Ideology, Salado Polychrome Pottery.* Univ. of New Mexico Press. Albuquerque, NM.

Cunkle, James R.
1993   *Talking Pots, Deciphering the Symbols of a Prehistoric People.* Golden West Pub. Phoenix, AZ.
1994   *Treasures of Time, a Guide to Prehistoric Ceramics of the Southwest.* Golden West Pub. Phoenix, AZ.

Doore, Gary
1988   *Shaman's Path; Healing, Personal Growth and Empowerment.* Shambhala Pub., Inc. Boston

Dunne, Peter Masten
1968   *Black Robes in Lower California.* University of California Press. Berkeley, CA.

Eddy, John
1981   *Astroarchaeology. In Insights into the Ancient Ones.* Mesa Verde Press. Cortez, CO.

Eliade, Mircea
1964   *Shamanism; Archaic Techniques of Ecstasy.* Bollingen Series LXXVI. Princeton Univ. Press. Princeton, NJ.

Eliot, Alexander
1976   *The Universal Myths; Heroes, Gods, Tricksters and Others.* Penguin Books, Inc. New York.

Fewkes, Jesse Walter
1895   *Designs on Prehistoric Hopi Pottery.* Thirty-third Annual Report of the Bureau of American Ethnology. Government Printing Offices, Washington D.C. 1914-1924.

Fewkes, Jesse Walter (continued)
1914-1924 *The Mimbres, Art and Archaeology.* Avanyu Publishing Inc. Albuquerque, NM (1989 reprint).
1914-1924 *Tusayan Katcinas and Hopi Altars.* Avanyu Publishing, Inc. Albuquerque, NM (1990 reprint).
Frazer, James G.
1981   *The Golden Bough.* Crown Publishers Inc. 1993 Edition, Outlet Books Co. Inc. Random House, Avenel, NJ.
Grant, Campbell
1967   *Rock Art of the American Indians.* Outbooks, Golden, CO.
1978   *Canyon de Chelly: Its People and Its Rock Art.* University of Arizona Press. Tucson, AZ.
Grim, John A.
1983   *The Shaman; Patterns of Religious Healing Among the Ojibway Indians.* The Civilization of the American Indians Series. University of Oklahoma Press. Norman, OK.
Harris, Marvin
1983   *Cultural Anthropology.* Harper and Row Publishers. New York.
Haury, Emil W.
1978   *The Hohokam, Desert Farmers and Craftsmen. Excavations at Snaketown, 1964-1965.* University of Arizona Press. Tucson, AZ.
Hodge, Frederick W.
1907   *The Narrative of Alvar Nunez Cabeca de Vaca and the Narrative of the Expedition of Coronado, by Pedro de Castaneda. Spanish Explorers of the Southern United States, 1528-1543,* edited by Frederick W. Hodge and Theodore H. Lewis. Charles Scribner's and Sons, New York.
Jennings, Jesse D.
1989   *Prehistory of North America.* Mayfield Publishing Co. Mountain View, CA.
Johnson, Boma
1986   *Earth Figures of the Lower Colorado and Gila River Deserts: A Functional Analysis.* Arizona Archaeological Society. Phoenix, AZ.
Jung, C. G.
1959   *The Basic Writings of C. G. Jung.* Random House, Inc. New York.
Kabotie, Fred
1982   *Designs from the Ancient Mimbrenos with a Hopi Interpretation.* 2nd ed. Northland Press. Flagstaff, AZ.
LeBlanc, Steven A.
1983   *The Mimbres People, Ancient Pueblo Painters of the American Southwest.* Thames and Hudson Inc. New York.
Malotki, Ekkehart and Michael Lomatuway'ma
1987a   *Maawaw: Profile of a Hopi God.* Univ. of Nebraska Press (Am. Tribal Religions) vol. 11. Lincoln, NE.
1987b   *Stories of Maasaw; A Hopi God.* Univ. of Nebraska Press (Am. Tribal Religions vol. 10) Lincoln, NE.
Mallery, Garrick
1893   *Picture Writing of the American Indians.* Bureau of Ethnology, Tenth Annual Report. Government Printing Office. Washington D.C.
Martineau, LaVan
1987   *The Rocks Begin to Speak.* K.C. Publications. Las Vegas, NV.
Moulard, Barbara L.
1984   *Within the Underworld Sky. Mimbres Art in Context.* Twelvetrees Press. Pasadena, CA.
Neihardt, John G.
1932   *Black Elk Speaks; Being the Life Story of a Holy Man of 1988—the Oglala Sioux.* University of Nebraska Press. Lincoln, Nebraska (reprint 1988).
Parsons, Elsie Clews
1938   *The Humpbacked Flute Player of the Southwest.* American Anthropologist 40, no.2.
1939   *Pueblo Indian Religion.* University of Chicago Press. Chicago
Patterson, Alex
1992   *A Field Guide to Rock Art Symbols of the Greater Southwest.* Johnson Printing Co. Boulder, CO.
1994   *Hopi Pottery Symbols.* Johnson Books. Boulder, CO.

Renaud, Etienne B.
1948   *Kokopelli: A Study in Pueblo Mythology. Southwestern Lore* 14, no. 2.

Ritter, Dale W. and Eric W. Ritter
1973   *Prehistoric Pictography in North America of Medical Significance.* IXth International Congress of Anthropological and Ethnological Sciences. Chicago.

Robbins, R.R. and R. B. Westmoreland
        Unpublished. *Astronomical Imagery and Numbers in Mimbres Pottery.*

Rohn, Arthur H., William M. Ferguson, and Lisa Ferguson
1989   *Rock Art of Bandelier National Monument.* University of New Mexico Press. Albuquerque, NM.

Schaafsma, Polly
1980   *Indian Rock Art of the Southwest.* School of American Research. University of New Mexico Press. Albuquerque, NM.
1981   *Kachinas in Rock Art.* In; Journal of New World Archaeology.

Schaafsma, Polly and Curtis F. Schaafsma
1974   *Evidence for the Origins of Pueblo Kachina Cult as Suggested by Southwestern Rock Art.* American Antiquity 39 (4):535-545.

Sims, Agnes C.
1963   *Rock Carvings: A Record of Folk History. In Sun Father's Way,* by Bertha Dutton. University of New Mexico Press. Albuquerque, NM.

Slifer, Dennis and James Duffield
1994   *Kokopelli, Flute Player Images in Rock Art.* Ancient City Press Santa Fe. NM.

Smith, Watson
1952   *Kiva Mural Decorations at Awatovi and Kawaika-a.* Peabody Museum. Cambridge, MA.

Stephen, Alexander MacGregor
1890   *Pottery of Tusayan*, Catalogue of the Keam Collection, unpublished manuscript.
1936   *Hopi Journal of Alexander M. Stephen vols. 1 and 2.* Columbia Univ. Contributions to Anthropology. Edited by Elsie Clews Parsons. Reprint 1969. AMS Press Inc. New York.

Stevenson, Matilda Coxe
1902   *The Zuni Indians.* 23rd Annual Report, Bureau of American Ethnology, Washington, D.C.

Tyler, Hamilton A.
1979   *Pueblo Birds and Myths.* Northland Publishing. Flagstaff, AZ.

Vastokas, Joan M. and Romas K. Vastokas
1973   *Sacred Art of the Algonkians: A Study of the Peterborough Petroglyphs.* Mansard Press. Peterborough, Ontario.

Vuncannon, Delcie H.
1985   *Fertility Symbolism at the Chalfant Site, California. Rock Art Papers vol. 2.* San Diego Museum of Man. San Diego, CA.

Wallace, Henry D., and James P. Holmlund
1986   *Petroglyphs of the Picacho Mountains: South Central Arizona.* Institute for American Research, Anthropological Papers 6.

Waters, Frank
1963   *The Book of the Hopi.* Viking Press. New York.

Webb, G. B.
1936   *Tuberculosis. In Clio Medico,* ed. E.G. Krumbhaar. Paul B. Hoeber, Inc. New York.

Williamson, Ray A.
1984   *Living the Sky: The Cosmos of the American Indian .* University of Oklahoma Press, Norman, OK.

Young, Dudley
1991   *Origins of the Sacred; The Ecstasies of Love and War.* (reprint1992). Harper Collins Publishers, Inc. New York.

Young, Jane M.
1988   *Signs From the Ancestors: Zuni Cultural Symbolism and Perceptions of Rock Art.* (reprint 1990). University of New Mexico Press, Albuquerque. NM.

Zigmond, Maurice L.
1977   *The Supernatural World of the Kawaiisu.* In *Flowers of the Wind: Papers on Ritual, Myth and Symbolism in California and the Southwest.* Ballena Press Anthropological Papers.

Index to Bibliographical References

— INDEX —

James Cunkle in the White Mountain Archaeological Center museum.

About

James R. Cunkle

As a boy James Cunkle traveled with his father into remote areas of the Southwest. As a teenager he traveled alone over hundreds of miles of wilderness and discovered prehistoric caves, petroglyphs and archaeological sites that were as yet unrecorded.

In 1988 he graduated Cum Laude and received a B.A. in Anthropology/Archaeology from Cleveland State University, Cleveland Ohio.

He is now the Coordinator and Director of Research of the White Mountain Archaeological Center of St. Johns, Arizona. Among his many accomplishments for the center he is especially proud of the ethnobiological gardens which have recently been developed. James has authored two other books about the discoveries at the archaeological center, *Talking Pots, Deciphering the Symbols of a Prehistoric People* and *Treasures of Time, A Guide to Prehistoric Ceramics of the Southwest.* Both books are published by Golden West Publishers.

Markus Jacquemain

About

Markus A. Jacquemain

For the better part of two decades, Markus Jacquemain has participated in and studied cultural organizations, from Mayan villages to modern religious/cult organizations.

Earning his B.A. degree in religious studies with an anthropological focus (Cleveland State University) has allowed him to concentrate on the anthropological study of the religious components of cultures, particularly with regard to Native American religious history. Markus recently led a hiking expedition which retraced ancient Indian pilgrimage trails over 240 miles through the Mohave desert.

Markus is currently preparing a work designed to assist in self-creation based on mythological archetypes and historical spiritual practices.

About the
White Mountain Archaeological Center

The White Mountain Archaeological Center is a non-profit facility that was created to protect and preserve prehistoric sites in the White Mountains of east/central Arizona. The Center directs the excavations at Raven Site Ruins and curates the cultural material from the site. The Center offers hands-on archaeological excavation, lab work and survey into the petroglyph areas illustrated in this book to anyone with an interest in the archaeological sciences. The Center is open from May through October. Daily, multiple day and week long programs are available. On site lodging is available by reservation.

The on site museum displays the cultural material discovered at Raven Site, and all of the artifacts are held in the repository at the same location. It is a rare opportunity to view all of the cultural material from a prehistoric pueblo in one place. If you would like to participate in the excavations, laboratory projects, or petroglyph surveys at the White Mountain Archaeological Center, call or write to make reservations for your program. Your interest and excitement provides the means and the method for our continuing research.

The petroglyph areas and shrine sites illustrated in this book can be visited and experienced by contacting the Center. Small groups are guided to the sites where you will share the excitement of the power of the place and the thrill of discovery. Visiting the petroglyph sites with small respectful groups increases the stewardship of these sensitive areas and decreases the mindless vandalism and petroglyph theft that is rapidly destroying a wealth of prehistoric symbolism.

By participating in the petroglyph survey programs at the Center you become an important part of the preservation process.

White Mountain Archaeological Center
H C 30, Box 30
St. Johns, Arizona 85936
520-333-5857

Also by James R. Cunkle . . .

TREASURES OF TIME

A Guide to Prehistoric Ceramics of the Southwest

A user-friendly guide to the ceramics that have been unearthed at Raven Site Ruins in northeastern Arizona. Author/archaeologist James R. Cunkle categorizes the primary groups of prehistoric ceramics found at the site and treats each in a separate chapter of in-depth information. Includes full-color insert, glossary and index.

6 x 9 — 216 Pages . . . $14.95

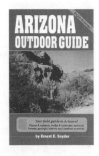

ORDER BLANK

GOLDEN WEST PUBLISHERS

☼ 4113 N. Longview Ave. • Phoenix, AZ 85014

602-265-4392 • **1-800-658-5830** • FAX 602-279-6901

Qty	Title	Price	Amount
	Arizona Cook Book	5.95	
	Arizona Crosswords	4.95	
	Arizona Museums	9.95	
	Arizona Outdoor Guide	6.95	
	Cactus Country	6.95	
	Chili-Lovers' Cook Book	5.95	
	Cowboy Slang	5.95	
	Discover Arizona!	6.95	
	Easy RV Recipes	6.95	
	Explore Arizona!	6.95	
	Fishing Arizona	6.95	
	Hiking Arizona	6.95	
	Hiking Arizona II	6.95	
	Horse Trails in Arizona	9.95	
	Motorcycle Arizona!	9.95	
	Prehistoric Arizona	5.00	
	Quest for the Dutchman's Gold	6.95	
	Salsa Lovers Cook Book	5.95	
	Scorpions and other Venomous Insects	9.95	
	Snakes and other Reptiles of the SW	9.95	
	Stone Magic of the Ancients	14.95	
	Talking Pots	19.95	
	Treasures of Time	14.95	
	Verde River Recreation Guide	6.95	

Add $2.00 to total order for shipping & handling $2.00

☐ My Check or Money Order Enclosed. . . . . $_____
☐ MasterCard   ☐ VISA   (Payable in U.S. funds)

Acct. No. _____ Exp. Date _____

Signature _____

Name _____ Telephone _____

Address _____

City/State/Zip   **Call for FREE catalog**

9/95   MasterCard and VISA Orders Accepted ($20 Minimum)
This order blank may be photo-copied.

Magic

Golden West's specialty is the Southwest!

✦ Characters and legends of the Wild West!

✦ Prospecting, hiking, fishing, horseback riding, hunting and much more!

✦ Southwestern cook books! Salsas, chilis, Mexican foods and other great tastes.

✦ State cook books! Try recipes from Washington, Oregon, Texas, Colorado, New Mexico and Arizona.

✦ Christmas cook books! Christmas recipes, traditions and folklore from Arizona, Colorado, Texas, Washington, and New Mexico!

✦ Southwestern guide books! Trees, cactus, mammals, birds, fossils, desert survival, venomous snakes and insects. Don't travel without them!

✦ Children's activity books. Games, crafts, educational information about our Southwestern states.

Call 1-800-658-5830 and place your order today!